YOU HAVE INFINITE POWER

YOU HAVE INFINITE POWER

ULTIMATE SUCCESS THROUGH ENERGY, PASSION AND PURPOSE

CHRIS BERLOW   PAUL MELELLA JR.   NICK PALUMBO   RICK WOLLMAN

EMPOWERED MASTERY
Your Life   Our Passion   One Purpose

528 North State Rd, Braircliff Manor, NY 10510

Previously published in 2010 by TechPress, Inc.

ISBN-13: 978-0692959152

For information about custom editions, special sales, and premium
and corporate purchases, please contact Empowered Mastery at
914-488-5881 or info@empoweredmastery.com.

empoweredmastery.com

— PRAISE FOR *YOU HAVE INFINITE POWER* —

You Have Infinite Power is more than just a powerful book: It's a must read for anyone from corporate executives to sales professionals and entrepreneurs who want to improve both their personal and professional lives. The authors not only share stories about their successes, they speak compellingly about their failures, offering invaluable insights on what they learned and how they adapted and recovered from these experiences. This is an inspiring, motivating, and timely work.

—Dennis J. Manning, president and chief executive officer, The Guardian Life Insurance Company of America

The consultants at Empowered Mastery helped my team of district managers look at their business in a new and opportunistic way. Corporations often teach leadership and management skills, but rarely help leaders frame their thinking for a more successful outcome. This book will help everyone who reads it become more successful both personally and professionally.

—Beth Nottingham, former vice president of Borders Books

You Have Infinite Power is helpful and easy to read, yet profound. It's loaded with practical advice, inspiration, and encouragement. The T.R.A.N.S.F.O.R.M.A.T.I.O.N. Doctrine provides a wealth of insights on improving your life.

—Jack Canfield, co-author of the Chicken Soup for the Soul series

Paul, Rick, Chris, and Nick's personal accounts of their obstacles and hardships are fabulous examples of how they overcame adversity and triumphed in life. That's what makes this book so great; these guys are real-life examples of, 'If I can do it, anybody can do it.'

—Marty Lyons, former professional football player and current announcer

Empowered mastery understands success. These four men, each of whom has forged his own successful path, offer something for everyone. Their diverse backgrounds blend together beautifully, giving the reader a realistic view of what it takes to transform your life.

—*James Ienner, award-winning movie and music producer*

Having gone to three Empowered Mastery events in the past year, I couldn't wait to read their book. They each had a dramatic effect on my personal and professional life. It provided me an opportunity to shed my emotional baggage and achieve tremendous psychological and physical breakthroughs.

I would recommend that anyone who is looking to make an impact in his or her life, and wants to increase productivity in their professional and personal life, read *You Have Infinite Power* and consider the EMC programs.

—*Paul Vecchione, financial advisor, Amper Financial Services, Bridgewater, NJ*

DEDICATIONS

This book is dedicated in loving memory of my little brother, Frank Palumbo Jr., who taught me how to laugh and enjoy life to the fullest. I will always cherish our memories. I will always feel your love through your children Katie, Frankie, and Sabrina. I also dedicate this book to my wife Linda and my beautiful children Joseph and Lia. I hope that the principles of this book will guide you.

—Nick

To my childhood best friend: John T. Furst III. His love for life was unparalleled, and his spirit will live on forever.

To my oldest brother, David Berlow, who was only with us for a little while but accomplished so much. He is still an inspiration with all his accomplishments.

To my mother, Ann Delano who passed away in 2010. I will love you forever and you will always be an inspiration for me and many generations to come. Your legacy of love and selflessness will live on forever.

—Chris

This book is dedicated in loving memory of my childhood best friend Michael Lubbers, who inspired me to think big, to take action, and to live life to the fullest. You will forever be in our hearts.

—Paul

I would like to dedicate this book to my parents, Elaine and Edward Wollman, who passed on years ago. As I get older, and as the years go by raising a family of my own, I come to understand and appreciate just how good my parents were. As often is the case, we don't realize the values our parents instill in us until we become parents ourselves.

My parents were fair, honest, humble, loving, and always supportive; these are qualities that every parent should have. I was extremely fortunate to be the recipient of their good nature. If I can be half the parent to my kids that they were to me, then I would consider myself extremely fortunate. They are my true heroes.

—Rick

CONTENTS

FOREWORD

You Have Infinite Power is the pinnacle of personal growth and development books. Within these pages, Nick, Chris, Paul, and Rick introduce their patented and groundbreaking T.R.A.N.S.F.O.R.M.A.T.I.O.N. Doctrine™, which will transform your life. *You Have Infinite Power* is a fourteen-step process that allows you to operate at peak performance in all areas of your life, whether personal or professional. These four authors and entrepreneurs come from diverse backgrounds and experiences, and have expertise in a variety of industries, which offers the reader a unique vantage point. Each of them has experienced success in his chosen endeavors by pursuing his dreams relentlessly and overcoming all obstacles in his path. They have, both individually and as a team, strived not only to succeed, but also to continually grow and evolve into an enlightened state that inspires their clients and those around them to reach their true potential.

Bookstore shelves are filled with books whose authors promise the new miracle cure for your life, but seldom do these authors walk their walk and talk their talk. While reading *You Have Infinite Power*, you will notice almost from the start that this book is different than any other book out there. Through personal stories of triumph and tragedy, the readers will come to feel as though they have known these men all their lives. Their openness and willingness to share their life experiences are a true testament to the genuine concern they have for their readers and clients. *You Have Infinite Power* encourages and inspires you to achieve what you never thought possible.

—Bob Proctor

The power and value of a Mastermind group has been proven time and time again. In *You Have Infinite Power*, these four dynamic authors have created a mastermind group to guide you on your own journey to success. They have combined their passion, purpose, and personal success to create the groundbreaking T.R.A.N.S.F.O.R.M.A.T.I.O.N. Doctrine, a fourteen-step process that trains your mind and enables you to operate at a peak performance and efficiency in all areas of your personal and professional life.

Nick Palumbo, Rick Wollman, Chris Berlow, and Paul Melella are alike in their passion, but different in their diverse backgrounds and unique abilities. Melella was trained in the martial arts field, and his vision and worthy ideal in life is to positively impact the lives of others. In fact, he signs his email with the signature, "live life to the fullest." He spent a decade traveling the world listening to the leaders in the personal development and self-improvement fields.

Melella found a kindred spirit in Palumbo, a well-respected leader in the financial services industry, who was training at his martial arts studio. Together they recognized an immediate synergy and common vision as well as an opportunity to create a unique approach to personal development and success.

Melella recruited Berlow, his lifelong friend and martial arts partner, while Palumbo invited Wollman, a successful entrepreneur and a friend for thirty years. Their commitment to excellence helped make the T.R.A.N.S.F.O.R.M.A.T.I.O.N. Doctrine and this book a reality. In discussing the power of collaboration I often say that $1 + 1 = 11$. In this combined effort by these four individuals $1 + 1 + 1 + 1$ truly does equal 1111!!!

There is no shortage of self-help books promising you a new life. Usually they are written from a single author's perspective. *You Have Infinite Power* shares the vantage points of four authors, each sharing with you their personal stories of not only their triumphs, but also their trials and struggles and how they persevered.

The men are open and candid, and have pursued their dreams and reached their successes using the same principles and fundamentals they share in this book.

They promise no miracles. They do promise that if you commit yourself to this process you will find growth and improvement in your life. Are you ready to find your ultimate success?

—Sharon Lechter,
Co-author of Three Feet from Gold and Rich Dad, Poor Dad;
Member of the First President's Advisory Council on Financial Literacy;
Founder and CEO of Pay Your Family First

Life isn't about waiting for storms to pass, but learning how to dance in the rain. Hopefully, with this book you'll come away with a few new steps.

—Anonymous

INTRODUCTION

What makes *You Have Infinite Power* different than other books? We do. The four of us came together with a purpose that led to the formation of Empowered Mastery and, ultimately, the T.R.A.N.S.F.O.R.M.A.T.I.O.N. Doctrine™. This is such a powerful process that we trademarked it. With our individual success and diverse backgrounds, we each have unique and uncommon qualities that appeal to a wide range of people. In most books, you only read one point of view. In *You Have Infinite Power*, four different outlooks on life come together to offer a wealth of knowledge and experience along with seventy conditioning exercises specifically designed to help you transform your life.

Our personalities are polar opposites, yet we all have the same core belief—we want to inspire others to transform their lives for the better. Nick owns a multimillion-dollar financial services business and is a sought-after platform speaker within his industry. Nick speaks from a wealth of knowledge, experience, and confidence from his success. Chris, an owner of a martial arts franchise, has unlimited energy and a relentlessly positive outlook on life. He has genuine trust and concern for others, which is evident in this book. Rick, a successful entrepreneur, is committed to excellence in all of his endeavors. His commitment and dedication keep us all aligned and focused. A day never passes when he isn't on top of his game. And Paul, an owner of the same martial arts franchise as Chris, has dedicated his life to this doctrine. As you will see, he is one of the most disciplined people you will ever come across. He sets an example for all who meet him. Enthusiasm radiates from him when he speaks, and his passion for health and vitality weave uniqueness into this book.

Other books claim to know all, to speak above you, and to promise untold riches, yet amazingly, their authors are rarely forthcoming about their own experiences. In this book, all four authors are just as willing to share their past failures as their past successes: Nick being on welfare and losing a son, Rick being fired twice, Chris coming from a broken family, Paul being faced with jail as a teenager. All successful people have experienced failure at some point during their lives, yet it is how we learn from these experiences and how we bounce back from them that hold the real key to success. So if you've been looking for something different, *You Have Infinite Power* is for you.

At our company, Empowered Mastery, we begin each of our seminars with the "Empty Your Cup" story. We would like to share this story with you. A college professor wanted to learn the art of Zen, so he searched for a Zen master to train under. Once he began training with the Zen master, he constantly interjected with comments. During each of his lessons, the college professor would interrupt the Zen master and say, "Well, this is what I was taught" or "I think this way is better." So one day the Zen master asked the college professor to join him for a cup of tea. They sat down, and the Zen master poured and poured and poured the tea into the professor's cup until it overflowed. The professor finally said to the Zen master, "Stop! What are you doing? The tea is overflowing all over the place." The Zen master said, "Like this cup, you are already filled with your own knowledge. I cannot teach you the art of Zen until you empty your cup." As you read these pages, empty your current mindset and be open to the ideas and theories presented to you.

Unlike other books, we at Empowered Mastery aren't here to say that our way is right and any other way of thinking is wrong. If you don't agree with some of our philosophies and theories, that's okay. All we ask is that you have an open mind, like in the story above. The techniques we describe transform thousands of lives each year through our seminars, workshops, and clients, as well as through the students we teach as martial artists. Each of us at one time or another has implemented the steps of the T.R.A.N.S.F.O.R.M.A.T.I.O.N. Doctrine in his life. We do practice what we preach, and we do walk the walk.

Now, we're extremely grateful to have the privilege to share these steps with you. Each time you read these chapters, you will learn something new. As a matter a fact, you will find that you will refer back to this book for many years to come. Feel free to highlight and mark it just as you did your old college textbooks. *You Have Infinite Power* is specially designed for the reader to easily navigate through the wealth of information within each chapter. In each chapter, you will find inspiring and motivating author stories. In these real-life, personal experiences, we share with you our greatest challenges and defining moments.

The material in this book is presented in an easy-to-read format that you can digest at your own pace. Each time you read these chapters, you will find some new nuggets of information helpful to your life.

Quotations. At the beginning of each chapter, you will find inspiring quotations from famous individuals to help set the tone for each step of our T.R.A.N.S.F.O.R.M.A.T.I.O.N. Doctrine.

Empowering Statements. We believe these statements are so strong and so powerful that we've highlighted them throughout the book.

Conditioning for Success Exercises. These exercises were carefully created to help you, the reader, get a clearer insight and understanding about who you are and how to implement each step of the T.R.A.N.S.F.O.R.M.A.T.I.O.N. Doctrine.

Chapter Summary. These offer a quick synopsis for each step presented throughout the chapter.

CHAPTER ONE

Thought

{
We are what we think. All that we are arises
with our thoughts. With our thoughts, we
make our world.

–BUDDHA
}

What if we told you that you had exactly the same
abilities and resources that most successful people have?
What if we told you that developing a totally different IQ
is the key to prosperity and happiness? It's not the Intelligence Quotient that we are referring to; it's what we
call the Intellectual Qualities (IQ) that hold the key. The
good news about this IQ is that, unlike the other where
there are indeed differences from one person to another,
we are all born with these intellectual qualities. No one
person has more than any other.

We all have infinite ability. We all have genius within us. Bill Gates, Steve Jobs, Oprah Winfrey, and the overwhelming majority of successful people throughout history were not born with any more ability or gifts than anyone else, but as they matured they learned to develop their IQ. They just believed they could do certain things. Once you learn to develop these resources, you will manifest almost every goal imaginable. Your health will improve, your professional life will soar, and your relationships will be more fulfilling. Most things in life are possible as long as you truly believe in yourself and your capabilities.

You are your thoughts!

Everything starts with a thought. Any thought that enters your mind, whether positive or negative, can become reality if you so choose. This is the foundation for the remaining chapters in this book. Intellectual Qualities go beyond the five senses of touch, taste, smell, vision, and hearing. Your IQ is your innate ability to manifest your desires into reality. This does not mean all you have to do is close your eyes and say, "I want to be a millionaire," and in a blink of an eye you'll be on a yacht in Monte Carlo sipping martinis. No, it's not that easy. However, do not underestimate the power of your mind, and the potential of any thought you put into it.

The Intellectual Qualities are
- Imagination
- Confidence
- Optimism
- Desire (burning)
- Passion
- Commitment
- Faith
- Vision
- Living through your worthy ideal

Our T.R.A.N.S.F.O.R.M.A.T.I.O.N. Doctrine guides you through the process of understanding and developing your intellectual qualities and enabling you to reinvent yourself as the person you've dreamed of.

You may still not be convinced of the power of your own thoughts compared to the Bill Gateses and Steve Jobses of the world. They are examples of brilliant entrepreneurs, right? They are much smarter than the average person, right? Wrong! They both failed at one time or another. They both dropped out of college. One even got fired. We can venture to say that each of us has the same basic level of intellectual qualities that they have; it is how we choose to apply them that makes the difference. Bill Gates was at Harvard in 1975 when he first read an article about a new machine called the microcomputer. He was fascinated and made the decision almost immediately to design the best computer software in the world. We all know what followed. Microsoft's innovations have allowed people with no computer experience to use personal computers and lead the global software industry. The idea for the personal computer was already available, but Gates tapped into his IQ, opening his mind to vision and imagination in order to fuel his desire and passion to pursue and live through his Worthy Ideal of providing everyone with the opportunity to own a computer. In Chapter 3, we detail these intellectual qualities and their importance.

Stop and think for a moment about the different people in your life: your family, friends, coworkers, and acquaintances. When you think about them, is there one who constantly communicates negative thoughts? How is their life? Are they happy? Healthy? We'd be willing to say that they are none of these things because they live their negative thoughts.

The universe is governed by thoughts; therefore, everything we are is a direct result of our thinking. To improve your results, you first must go to the source. The following illustration demonstrates the power of your thoughts. It is so simple to understand yet so few people realize it let alone apply it into their daily lives.

We feel this formula is so important and so crucial to people's success that we called this the Empowered Mastery Success Formula.

Thoughts $\longrightarrow$ Feelings/Emotions $\longrightarrow$ Actions $\longrightarrow$ Results

Results are what we want to improve in our lives, so if you want to improve your results, simply change your thoughts. Whatever we think about can become a reality. Why then do we fill our minds with negative thoughts? Why do we always think of reasons why we can't do something instead of why we can? Understanding the mind enables us to learn to develop the right mindset to overcome any obstacle, accomplish any feat, or achieve any goal. Once you've changed your thinking, you can transform daily actions and break free of limiting behaviors that hold you back. Before we can go any further into the importance of thought, we need to first discuss the inner workings of your mind.

Now don't worry, you won't have any nightmarish flashbacks of chemistry class. No need to get out your textbooks. There won't be too much medical jargon here. After all, we aren't brain surgeons, but what we talk about here is just as important and easier to understand.

Okay, so let's get started. Every thought in the mind triggers a chemical and neurological process and creates different pathways in the brain. Each person develops unique patterns of connections between brain cells. As you tap into the power of these patterns and adjust your thinking, you gain a new, positive perspective. This process involves exchanging self-defeating thoughts and bad habits for more empowering and enabling ideas.

The brain contains ten to fifteen billion neurons. These neurons transmit information around your body and form connections between cells. The connections or neural pathways are similar to the interstate highway system that links the country together. Chemicals are released with connections between neurons. The more each connection is used, the more its pathway develops. A lifetime of negative and self-sabotaging thoughts can actually alter your neurons.

A good illustration of this is the path created by walkers in a park. Initially, an area may be lush and green. As time passes, the constant walking back and forth wears away the grass; with each step, a path becomes easier to see. Similarly, neural connections develop within the brain through thoughts, actions, or behaviors. The more often the thought occurs or the action is carried out, then the more the connections and pathways develop so that the action becomes much easier, more familiar, and eventually becomes a habit. Every time you repeat the habit, the connection becomes that much stronger within the brain, and it eventually becomes second nature to you—well worn, like the path we created in the park.

Is it possible to change behaviors by changing your thinking process? Can you actually re-wire your thinking? Absolutely! Decide what behavior you would like to change to have a positive effect on your life. To do so, it is necessary to develop a new connection in the brain and a new positive thought. For example, "I will stop eating unhealthy foods and go to the gym three times a week" or "I will replace my negative self-talk with encouraging statements." Instead of telling yourself, "I can't," say "I can." The more the positive thought is repeated, the more the new brain connection is reinforced. As a result, the old habits are changed. These new thought processes and behavioral changes need to be regularly repeated to strengthen the connection. It is estimated that it takes twenty-one days to develop a new habit and create new neural pathways. As a word of caution: be aware of your thoughts. Do they help or hinder you? Do you need to exchange some negative thoughts for more positive ones? Consider what habits you could change to keep your brain active and stimulated.

For the next twenty-one days, begin to create a new habit and new neural pathways. You need to carry out this new behavior several times. For example, when you wake up every morning, eat fresh, organic fruit and drink bottled water instead of coffee and doughnuts. As you eat the fruit and drink the water, say to yourself, "I feel great," "I am healthy, vital, and full of energy!" These statements are what we call power paradigms, which we will detail in the next chapter. As the new behavior is repeated, the brain connection becomes stronger, thereby creating a new habit and a neural pathway.

> It is only through your conscious mind that you can reach the subconscious. Your conscious mind is the porter at the door, the watchman at the gate. It is to the conscious mind that the subconscious looks for all its impressions.
>
> —ROBERT COLLIER

With apologies to Mr. Albert Einstein, we like to use the following equation to illustrate how your mind works.

EMPOWERMENT = MENTAL CAPACITY^2

We all have two minds, the conscious and subconscious, each with distinct attributes and powers. With the correct understanding of the purpose and functions of both, you will attract to yourself the circumstances and conditions most desired for your life. The best results are obtained through a close harmony and cooperation between the conscious and subconscious minds.

When we were kids, our parents or teachers told us that we could accomplish anything if we put our mind to it. The problem with that well-meaning statement is that we were never taught how to put our mind to it. We were never told how our mind works. Fortunately, we don't need to be a brain surgeon to understand how our mind works in relation to success.

> Man's task is to become conscious of the contents that
> press upward from the unconscious.
>
> —CARL GUSTAV JUNG

As Professional Martial Artists who have impacted thousands of students over the years, we realized that we did impact them, but never knew why. It is through the study of how the mind works that we realized why we are so successful in teaching our students. Martial arts training utilizes repetition and impact to allow beneficial values to sink into the student's subconscious mind. When this occurs, it dramatically effects their actions; the way they stand, sit, speak, and eat, their lifestyle, and all aspects of their lives. The results of their newfound lifestyle are remarkable. Children get better results in school and are more respectful at home, while adults earn promotions, feel calmer, and live healthier lives, all starting from the way they think.

Mental Capacity (Your Conscious Mind)

The conscious mind is the portion of your mind that utilizes sight, touch, sound, smell, and taste. It is also responsible for our ability to analyze thoughts and experience physical activity. We have complete control over the conscious portion of our minds. It can accept or reject any thought or outside influence. This is the thinking part of our minds.

Additionally, our conscious minds have the ability to form perceptions, whether true or false, according to our beliefs. We take these perceptions as reality. For example, if your parents gave you comfort food every time you cried or felt sad, then you may have a tendency to eat when a stressful situation occurs. Because of this limiting thought, you feel the need to comfort yourself with food. Your perceptions define your actions throughout the course of your life.

Effectively developing the powers of your conscious mind allows you to focus and dramatically enhances your life far beyond what you might consciously believe to be possible. Once the powers of your conscious mind are harnessed, you are able to filter out any negative or sabotaging thoughts or perceptions that have been predetermined by your subconscious mind. We have the ability to accept, reject, or neglect any thought that enters our conscious minds. However, when you don't learn how to take control over your conscious mind, then you allow your subconscious mind to form perceptions that can negatively affect your life, as the example of stress eating illustrates. Once you consciously choose to change your thoughts, your life will be filled with endless possibilities. When you become purposefully aware of your thoughts, you will then be able to choose only those thoughts that bring you empowerment. This is a key IQ ingredient that you must learn to develop and use.

Here are 8 simple words that will literally change your life. These 8 words are so simple to understand yet so few people actually apply them.

You Have the Ability to Choose Your Thoughts

Think about it. Only we can choose how we think, feel and act. Our physical bodies can be diseased, ill or broken down but we still have the ability to choose our thoughts.

People around us, from family and friends to our bosses and co-workers can try to influence how we think, but at the end of the day we have control, not them.

Successful people have the ability to choose their thoughts no matter the surroundings or challenges they may face. We are not saying it's always going to be easy, and sometimes we just blurt things out. We are not robots—we have feelings and emotions.

Choosing your thoughts enables you to erase old, self-defeating thoughts and to replace them with new and encouraging thoughts in your subconscious. You will no longer be a victim of your negative perceptions. You have the ability to control the information transmitted to your subconscious mind by choosing what you allow into your conscious mind.

66 We were giving a three-hour seminar for teachers at a New York City public school. We arrived early, and Chris proceeded to set up the computer and projector. Twenty minutes before the seminar was to begin, the projector stopped working. As we got closer to the starting time, I became angry and frustrated, not only at the projector but also at the attitudes of my partners. We were scheduled to start in a few minutes, the equipment wasn't working, and they didn't seem to care. I was focused on my negative thoughts, while Chris was focusing on a solution. Paul had complete faith in Chris and made better use of his time by focusing his thoughts in a positive and productive way: preparing for the seminar and establishing the right mindset. Their thought process was calmness, while mine was panic. As it turned out, Chris solved the problem just minutes before the seminar was to begin. I learned a valuable lesson from Paul and Chris that day: you and you alone have the power to choose your thoughts. Simply put, you can choose to be negative, or you can choose to be positive. Your actions and consequently your results are a direct correlation of your thoughts. 99

—RICK

Only one thing registers on the subconscious mind: repetitive application—practice. What you practice is what you manifest.

—FAY WELDON

Mental Capacity (Your Subconscious Mind)

Your subconscious mind is your emotional or feeling mind. It only has the ability to accept information the conscious mind gives it and is most impacted both before you go to sleep at night and when you wake up in the morning. We mentioned earlier the twenty-one days it takes to break a habit. Most people wake up in the morning and have a cup of coffee. Some have several. Instead, consciously choose to drink a bottle of water or green tea.

The effects of anesthesia provide a striking example of the power of your subconscious mind. The common perception of the purpose of anesthesia is that it stops pain or immobilizes the patient. Yes, it does this, but it also controls your body and its defense mechanisms that deal with pain. Anesthesia blocks your conscious awareness of the pain. You don't remember it, and therefore you don't relive it in your mind.

Your subconscious mind primarily controls your unconscious bodily functions, such as heartbeat and breathing. It also acts as a storage unit for all of the information received through your conscious mind. Your subconscious mind never sleeps. It works continuously, soaking up your conscious thoughts like a sponge. Before too long, that sponge becomes saturated and spills over into your reality. The subconscious mind can't distinguish the difference between true or false but acts only upon the thoughts given to it by the conscious mind.

Every thought given to your conscious mind repeatedly drops down into your subconscious mind and is accepted as truth. These thoughts are accepted as facts because your subconscious mind has no reasoning capability. Consequently, the negative thoughts you think about daily create self-defeating perceptions. These limiting beliefs may have been absorbed since childhood and accepted as truth. Many of them were innocently placed in your mind by well-meaning people who had no understanding of the power of the mind. How many times as a child did you hear statements like, "You can't do that," or "Stop daydreaming," or "You're just wasting your life away."

These beliefs fill your subconscious mind and determine your destiny. Now is the time to act. The only thought you should have in your subconscious mind is "anything is possible." For this reason, you absolutely must begin to selectively choose your thoughts. Once you are able to do this, then you can start to recognize and discern your current false and self-limiting perceptions from the real truth. Any negative and self-deprecating thoughts are stored and held as truth by your subconscious mind, no matter how wrong they may be. These self-limiting, pre-programmed beliefs are false beliefs that keep you from living the life you deserve.

66 My brother was told at a very early age that he wouldn't be any good at sports because of his limited mobility. He had to take occupational therapy when he was a child due to a lack of coordination and motor skills. He began martial arts at the age of four and began sparring competitions at the age of five. He was always smaller than the rest of his martial arts competitors but decided to compete anyway. When others told him he was learning disabled and had to take occupational therapy classes, I told him he could be a champion. When others told him he wasn't tall enough to be a champion, I told him he was faster than the competition. He didn't allow other people to limit his thinking; instead he believed what his older brother had been programming into his subconscious mind since the age of five, "You are a champion." At sixteen years old, he won the junior Olympic nationals, competed on a Junior National team, and won the Adult Men's Fin Weight National Championship. My brother learned to be a champion not only of martial arts, but also of his thoughts. 99

—PAUL

Your subconscious mind is a source of power for you. Stored deep within are the memories and experiences of your life. It is a tremendous source of energy that gives you the ability to develop strength, courage, and faith. It also embodies the feeling and wisdom of the past, the awareness and knowledge of the present, and the thought and vision of the future. Even though it is closely aligned to your physical body, your subconscious mind operates independently of the body. Below are seven key points to remember about your subconscious mind.

1. It manifests itself only according to your capabilities.
2. You must have a clear and vivid image of what you want and actually see yourself as already successful.
3. You must have patience and absolute faith. You must truly believe.
4. Your subconscious is only stable and effective in direct proportion to the quality and clarity of the information supplied to it by your conscious mind.

5. Your subconscious will draw to you what it clearly understands to be your desire.
6. Your subconscious doesn't reason why but records with high fidelity anything and everything your conscious mind presents to it.
7. You must ask it in detail exactly what you want. The mind can't process a negative, so keep your thoughts positive.

We know this has might have been a lot of information and it might be challenging to understand everything.

The illustration below will help you digest it more effectively. We use this in all of our seminars and workshops, and our clients have found it to be extremely effective.

Let's put the above illustration to use with something that all of us have done every single day for most of our lives: brushing our teeth. We first started doing this at a very young age because our parents told us to. Now, we weren't born with this idea, right? No, This thought was put into our conscious mind and through repetition and impact that thought of brushing our teeth seeped into our subconscious mind where we had the ability to accept that thought. And when we accepted that thought it became a habit.

Now that you have a better understanding of the roles that thought and belief play in your daily life, you need to determine exactly what you want. The general idea that you simply want to be successful is too vague. If your idea of success is to be wealthy, then you need to be able to have a specific amount of money in mind. If accomplishment is what you desire, then you need to define what your achievements will be. So, answer these three questions:

What is it I want?

_____

What are my exact goals?

_____

Do I have a clear picture in my mind of what I really want?

_____

These questions are crucial because the answers will determine your whole life from this point forward. How did you do with the above questions? Did you have any trouble with your answers? Did they make you feel uncomfortable? Strange as it may seem, these simple questions are very difficult for some people to answer. Most of us have a general desire to succeed, but beyond that, everything is unclear.

> **66** In 1976, I went to Italy to visit my relatives. I remember my uncle Frank asking me what I wanted to do with my life and then telling me that no matter what career I chose, I would make a lot of money. He gave me one thousand lire and told me, *Tanti bachi, zio Franco.* (Many kisses, Uncle Frank.) He asked me to turn the bill over and write, *Io Nicola dovo fare un milione di dolleri a cuarante ani.* (I Nick will earn a million dollars by the time I am forty.) In 2002, I turned forty and made a million dollars. I still carry those one thousand lire with me today. **99**

—NICK

It is vital that you know exactly what you want out of life. Your future has to be outlined, and your goals kept in view. You must have a set mental picture before you'll obtain the life of your dreams. Desire is the main motivating force in all of us, and it must be all consuming. Nothing can be achieved or gained without it. Combining the power of your thoughts with a deep burning desire is the prescription for getting whatever you want in life. Our thoughts and wants do not become real to us until we give them life with our own thinking or through the workings of our imaginations. We will delve deeper into imagination in Chapter 12.

> Man's greatness lies in his power of thought.
>
> —BLAISE PASCAL

The Power of your Thoughts

We have approximately sixty thousand thoughts every day. How many of those thoughts do you suppose are negative or self-defeating? Would you associate with someone who repeatedly told you how terrible you were all day long? If not, then why do you do it to yourself? Sadly, most of us go through our lives totally unaware of the power of our thoughts to produce the lives we desire. Worse yet, most of us aren't even consciously aware of what we're thinking in the first place! The majority of our thoughts are unconscious. Not being aware of them opens the door wide for an unwelcome, unwanted, and misunderstood life.

We can gain power over our thoughts once we learn to become aware of them. You have control; they don't have control over you. How many times have we heard uplifting stories about people who refuse to give in to sickness, illness, or other devastating obstacles put in their path? How many times have we heard that these people changed how they thought? Your thoughts shape your reality.

Here's another example of how powerful our thought processes can be: the work of Japan's Dr. Masaru Emoto. Over the past few years, Dr. Emoto has experimented with the effects of ideas, words, and music on the molecules of water. He froze and then photographed untreated, distilled water. The different samples of frozen, distilled water showed various formations, but none were crystallized. Next, he taped certain words or people's names on the outside of the bottles and subjected them to different types of music before freezing. Here are some effects that Dr. Emoto claims to have found in his research:

- Water from clear mountain springs and streams formed beautiful crystalline structures, while the crystals of polluted or stagnant water were deformed and distorted.
- Distilled water exposed to classical music took on delicate, symmetrical crystalline shapes.
- When the words "thank you" were taped to a bottle of distilled water, the frozen crystals had a similar shape to the crystals formed by water exposed to Bach's "Goldberg Variations."
- When Elvis Presley's "Heartbreak Hotel" was played to water, the resulting frozen crystals split in two.
- When water samples were bombarded with heavy metal music or labeled with negative words, or when negative thoughts and emotions were focused intentionally upon them, the water did not form crystals at all but displayed chaotic, fragmented structures.
- When water was treated with aromatic floral oils, the water crystals tended to mimic the shape of the original flower.
- When the words "Adolf Hitler" were taped to a bottle of distilled water, the crystals were fragmented and distorted.
- When the words "You fool" were taped to a container of distilled water, the crystals were almost identical to the formation that emerged when heavy metal music was played.
- When the words "Let's do it" were taped to a bottle of distilled water, beautiful, snowflake-like crystals formed, yet when the words "Do it" were taped to the distilled water, no crystals were produced at all.

Many of you may be skeptical of these experiments. Whether you choose to believe the photographs or not depends on your willingness to open your mind to new avenues of thinking and emptying your cup. At the very least, do an online search for Dr. Emoto and form your own conclusions.

We hope to have given you a new avenue to consider as you begin your travels through the power of thought. The amazing images of crystal formations are proof that the thought of failure itself can become represented in the physical objects that surround us. Now that we have seen this, perhaps we can begin to realize that even when immediate results are invisible to the unaided human eye, they are there. Our bodies at birth are 70 percent water; this percentage of water remains high throughout life (depending upon weight and body type). This means our bodies largely respond to these same influences.

The earth's surface is also 70 percent water. Through Dr. Emoto's experiments, we have seen the proof that water is far from inanimate and is actually alive and responsive to our every thought and emotion. Having seen this, perhaps we can begin to truly understand the awesome power that we possess, through choosing our thoughts and intentions, to heal the earth and ourselves. If those crystals can form in nature and water, then what is forming in your body? How are your crystals? Pristine? Beautiful? Or discolored and misshapen?

This is where you need to change your thought process. Thoughts and beliefs of lack and limitation have a negative effect. We would like to take this opportunity to state that not everyone's circumstances in life result from thoughts of lack and limitation. In some instances, such as war, a person's suffering has nothing to do with his or her thoughts. For the majority of people, however, until they are able to change the initial thought processes that created the situation, they will continue to experience the same results and will remain stuck in the same unsatisfying life. Until your limiting thought process changes, you will continue to get the same results. Each one of us has the ability to think and create something every minute of every day.

One of the best examples of the mind's ability to overcome a horrific obstacle is that of Viktor Frankl. He was an Austrian psychiatrist and surgeon in the early twentieth century. In 1942, he, his wife, and his parents were sent to the Theresienstadt concentration camp. Frankl was separated from his family and forced to live in horrendous conditions with hundreds of other men. For three years, he endured inhumane treatment by the Nazis. Surrounded by death, he noticed that many of the men simply gave up on life. They essentially "willed" themselves to die.

Frankl not only survived this horrific experience but also helped others to survive as well. His will to see the meaning in life set an example for many of the men around him. In his book *Man's Search for Meaning* he describes a time during his internment that nearly overwhelmed him. He was starving and suffering from many physical ailments. He wrote,

I became disgusted with the state of affairs which compelled me, daily and hourly, to think of such trivial things. I forced my thoughts to turn to another subject. Suddenly, I saw myself standing on the platform of a well lit, warm, and pleasant lecture room. In front of me sat an attentive audience on comfortable upholstered seats. I was giving a lecture on the psychology of the concentration camp! All that oppressed me at that moment became subjective, seen and described from the remote viewpoint of science. I succeeded somehow in rising above the situation, above the suffering of the moment, and I observed them as if they were already of the past.

By changing his thoughts, he was able to survive the horrors of the concentration camp. The next time you feel yourself slipping into a pattern of deprecating thoughts, think of Viktor Frankl and his ability to rise above the situation and think himself through one of the worst events of history. A more recent example is Nelson Mandela and his ability to remain positive throughout the 27 years he was imprisoned in very harsh conditions.

Another reason we need to truly understand the power of our thoughts is that often we may consciously desire one result, yet subconsciously be focused on another. As a result, due to the massive power of our thoughts, we experience more of our underlying subconscious desires. It is vital for you to understand that if you choose to have whatever you desire in life, then your predominant thoughts must be focused on and in harmony with what is desired and not what is lacking. The mind cannot process a negative. Most people are always focused on what they don't want, so if you say to yourself, "I don't want to be in debt," then your mind becomes focused on debt. What you really want is to be wealthy, so you change your thought to "I want to be financially free and abundant." At our seminars, we also hear our students say, "I just don't want to get sick." Their mind hears the word "sick," so we tell them to say, "I am healthy and vital" instead. What does your mind hear? The following exercise is useful in helping you determine how you want your life to be.

LIFE IS A BLANK CANVAS. YOU ARE THE PICASSO OF YOUR LIFE. TAKE A MOMENT AND USE THE SPACE BELOW TO DESIGN AN IDEAL LIFE. WRITE AND DESCRIBE EXACTLY WHAT YOU WANT YOUR LIFE TO BE LIKE.

Make a conscious effort, and you will develop the ability to focus the power of thoughts on creating a life far in excess of your previous comprehension. Now that you've discovered the power of thoughts, become conscious of what you are creating, and you will begin to experience a T.R.A.N.S.F.O.R.M.A.T.I.O.N. Learning to consciously implement the power of your thoughts is vital to achieving your dreams and goals. All that is necessary to attract your desire, whether it is financial security, incredible health, or fulfilling relationships, is to make a conscious choice to change and to replace the limited thinking that has stifled your life. Soon your life will be one of unimaginable success and empowerment.

CHAPTER SUMMARY

- We are all born with the same intellectual qualities to succeed.
- You have the ability to choose your thoughts.
- Your thoughts can alter the chemicals in your brain.
- You have complete control over your conscious mind.
- Any thought you repeat is automatically accepted into your subconscious mind.
- Your thoughts shape your reality.
- The conscious mind has the ability to accept, reject, or neglect any thought.
- Your conscious mind is your thinking mind.
- Your subconscious mind can only accept what it is given by your conscious mind.
- Your subconscious mind is your emotional or feeling mind.

CHAPTER TWO

Replacing Emotional Scars

{
The significant problems we face cannot be solved at the same level of thinking we were at when we created them.

—ALBERT EINSTEIN
}

As mentioned in Chapter 1, certain beliefs have been instilled in our subconscious as we matured. Many of the thoughts we have every day aren't ours. They didn't originate in our mind but are a product of those around us. The ideas of others far too often shape our world. As small children, the thoughts of our parents, teachers, coaches, and other influential people became our own. Similarly as adults, the things we read and watch have a dramatic impact on our thoughts. These external factors can have a damaging influence.

Are we born with a conscious mind? Most of us would answer yes. The question is not meant to be literal and analyzed by scientists, but rather food for thought. So let's propose another question: how do we as infants learn how to speak a language, while as adults we find it so difficult to learn a new one? When we are born we do not have the ability to agree or disagree. We don't have real opinions or original thought. We absorb everything around us like a sponge. As infants, we do not have a conscious mind, but we do have a subconscious mind that allows us to take things as they are. We have no choice but to accept what's around us. Therefore, we learn to speak the language in our environment. As we get older we start to form a conscious mind and therefore the ability to reject, accept or neglect what's around us. In other words, we have the ability to choose what's right for ourselves. That is why it's so challenging for us to learn a new language as adults. Our conscious mind gets in the way.

> 66 As a child I learned not only English but also Italian, which is the native language of my parents. I did not take Italian in school, I just picked it up from hearing my parents and relatives speak. My parents have been in this country for over 50 years, and they still speak broken English. Their conscious mind serves as their obstacle. 99
>
> —NICK

Before we can take one step forward to achieve what we want out of life, we have to take two steps back and take a look at how we got to this point in the first place. We all have what we call emotional scars. These are scars that developed in childhood and we didn't even realize we had. They are deep in our subconscious and might be standing in the way of achieving successes in our life. We have to unburden ourselves and replace these emotional scars. Before we can do that, we have to understand what these scars are and how they took up space in our subconscious.

Paradigms

Another word for emotional scars is paradigms. A paradigm is a set of beliefs and values that define the way a person views his or her reality. They control all behavior, which in turn propels results. It is crucial for us to learn that paradigms are formed and have a significant effect on our lives. In the first chapter, we detailed the importance of the power of your thoughts; now we apply that understanding to our paradigms. Only through this understanding can we transform paradigms to improve the way we think and act so as to bring about the most improved results. All of our results in life are based on our habits, attitudes, and, ultimately, our paradigms.

Our paradigms control almost every aspect of our lives and all the decisions we make on a daily basis, from

- Where we live
- Who we vote for
- How we invest our money
- Who we marry
- How we bring up our kids
- What books we read

These paradigms or perceptions control our expectations and determine how we interpret the events and circumstances in our life. On a scientific level (don't worry, we won't get technical here), paradigms control the way information is processed in our mind. The way we approach the world around us is a direct result of our paradigms. Paradigms are housed in our subconscious mind.

One of the most rewarding experiences we have as martial arts teachers is to see the transformation from the "non-believers" to the "Yes I can" mentality. A lot of beginner students' limitations come from their past. They lack the confidence and the belief that they could train in the martial arts. The biggest one is, "I am too old to train in the martial arts." Tell that to Chris's student who started her training at the age of 67 and is now on her way to earn a 3rd degree black belt at the age of 74. We tell our students, "If you don't do it, someone else will so it might as well be you."

> In every work of genius we recognize our own rejected thoughts.
>
> —RALPH WALDO EMERSON

Limiting Beliefs

Many people are convinced that their beliefs that result from their suffering, whether emotional, spiritual, or physical, are devastating beyond recovery. This is not the case.

No belief is permanent.

Most of us want to improve in order to reach our personal best. We think to ourselves, if only I could lose weight, or get a better job, or find a soul mate. But in the end, something always seems to stop us. Have you ever wondered why you don't get the results you want? Limiting beliefs determine your outcome. By integrating false beliefs with your actions, the results are detrimental. When you take time to comprehend this concept, your mindset shifts to one of unlimited possibility, and you put yourself in the position to achieve any result you choose. Let's take an example of the "check engine" light in a car. If it flashes red, do you take a hammer and bash the control panel until the light goes off? Of course not—that doesn't fix anything. More than this, just because the light is off doesn't mean the engine is now working correctly. Instead, you need to pull over, open the hood, and take a look inside. In other words, we need to treat the cause, not the symptom.

The same is true with life. Is your check engine light on? Something deep inside keeps us from changing. Something prevents us from believing in ourselves enough to reach our goals and fulfill our dreams. What is it? What keeps us from going back to school? Losing weight? Earning more money? It's simple really; if you don't believe you can do something, then your behavior will reflect that belief.

These beliefs can be traced back to our childhood. They are developed during a time when we did not have a fully developed conscious mind. We only had a subconscious mind which only allowed us to accept the thoughts of others. The worst part is that we carry these limited beliefs around, buried in our subconscious minds, for many years and don't even know they are there. We might simply accept them as our own beliefs. We are not saying that some of these beliefs aren't good, because they can be. We will dive more into this shortly when we talk about the different types of paradigms we have.

> Whether you think you can or think you can't, you're right.
>
> —HENRY FORD

Breaking free

You have to break free of limiting beliefs. Do you need to open your hood and give yourself an internal check up? Are your limiting beliefs holding you back?

In one way or another, these limiting beliefs affect every moment of life. Many of us find it difficult to break out and live the life we've always wanted. In our seminars, we teach our clients that the limiting beliefs that keep us from achieving our dreams are directly related to our childhoods. During our childhood, our feelings about ourselves were first formed. As we matured, these beliefs about our abilities—how we should act, how others perceive us, and most importantly, how we should behave—were reinforced as well. But just because your childhood is in the past doesn't mean it is over. Lingering childhood ideas, emotional scars, surface in our lives every day. Even as adults, our childhood experiences still affect us.

As a child, you might have felt unworthy, incompetent, inadequate, unlovable, or insignificant. This book is not about placing blame; it is about living the best life possible. You must take responsibility for your actions and life. Some of you may have been severely hurt by past events, but you can't continue to blame your current behaviors on someone else. How far can you drive forward by looking in the rear view mirror? Similarly, how far do you expect to move forward by living in the past? We cannot live in our past experiences. This hinders our progression. Leave the past where it belongs, in the past.

Instead, ask yourself, "What did I learn from that experience? What positives can I take from this?" At the same time, however, completely ignoring your past is not an option either. You can't go through life wearing blinders. To honestly improve your life, you must be willing to confront the past and to search for the cause of your limiting beliefs. No problem is fixable until there is a diagnosis. Can you imagine going to the doctor, only to be handed a diagnosis before your examination? You would probably walk straight out the door. Instead, the doctor asks for an explanation of symptoms, runs a few diagnostic tests, then prescribes medication. That is treating the symptoms instead of the cause. This could be one of the many reasons why we are an over-medicated society.

Guilt, anxiety, fear, low self-confidence, self-pity, and lack of self-esteem are traceable to childhood. These feelings seep over into our adult lives. We learned those feelings then and still apply them to our life now. All of our fears and worries were learned many years ago from various experiences, yet we continue to hold on to them. Most of our beliefs about who we are haven't changed at all since our formative years, so why do we still let them reign supreme over our lives? The answer is fear. Change is scary. Why do you think so many people get up year after year and go to jobs they dislike? Because they are too scared to change. I can't imagine letting fear steal happiness from me.

Don't let fear steal your happiness.

Most people fear the word "change." Change is constant; it's a universal law. The earth, the trees, the oceans, and mountains are all in a state of continuous change. Nothing remains still. Our bodies constantly change from birth to death. It's well known that every seven years all of the cells in our bodies are replaced. The world is forever evolving as well. For us to live a life of fulfillment and empowerment, then we need to embrace change as a positive. At Empowered Mastery, we believe the words "change" and "improve" are synonymous. No one wants to change for the worse; we all want to change for the better. Learn to dance with the fear of change and shift your mindset to create new possibilities in your life.

No one, no matter how strong or how smart, can move forward until they let go of their past. To do this, we must break free of our limiting beliefs and replace our emotional scars. Just by confronting negative, self-limiting beliefs, you have a much better chance of freeing yourself from fear and doubt. Stop allowing those negative ideas, which have been crowding your mind for too many years, to determine your behavior. Erase the messages that told you that you weren't good enough, smart enough, pretty enough, or anything else— they're ridiculous. To erase these, you have to go back in time—not literally of course—to your childhood and evaluate the standards you learned to judge yourself by.

Limiting beliefs are the culprit for the creation of what we call Paralyzing Paradigms. These hold you back from reaching your personal potential in life. They are the thoughts that prevented—and are still preventing you—from accomplishing your goals and reaching your dreams. Remember, you and you alone consciously choose your thoughts. Whatever thoughts you choose over and over again will be conditioned into your subconscious mind. This is where all your beliefs and paradigms are formed. Once a belief is formed into a paradigm and is conditioned into your subconscious mind, then it becomes reality. Every Paralyzing Paradigm has a polar opposite as well and can also be conditioned into our subconscious mind with what we call Power Paradigms. Power Paradigms are your empowering beliefs, which condition your mind for success. These empower you to be, to do, and to have whatever your heart desires. This is your natural state.

Your core beliefs have controlled you for a long time. Changing core beliefs opens the pathway for you to achieve whatever you desire. If you hold on to your old thought patterns, then nothing will improve. Unless your limiting beliefs change, your paradigms will plague you for the rest of your life. In order to improve, you need to create what we call a paradigm shift. You need to move from a constrictive negative energy to a positive energy that moves you forward. To change your paradigms, you must start from the inside.

Courageously analyze your beliefs one at a time. Ask yourself if these beliefs are truly yours, or someone else's, instilled in you since childhood. As you go through this process, you will find that many of your strongest convictions have no basis. Through careful review of your belief system, your existing paradigms will start to fade away and healthy, powerful ones will follow. This is the starting point for a better life.

In the space provided, list five Paralyzing Paradigms. After you've completed your list, make a second one replacing them with Power Paradigms.

PARALYZING PARADIGMS

Example. I am too old to begin that exercise program or it is too late to start a new career.

1.

2.

3.

4.

5.

POWER PARADIGMS

Example. I am healthy and vital and am in the best shape of my life!

1.

2.

3.

4.

5.

We've just learned that what we are and what we become is a direct result of our thoughts and beliefs. You are a direct reflection of those deeply embedded beliefs that have gradually, steadily, and consistently ingrained themselves into your psyche.

Things do not change; we change.

—HENRY DAVID THOREAU

Inside-Out

It is a universal law that everything grows from the inside out, including us. Let's put this to the test. What is the most common New Year's resolution? To lose weight and exercise, right? So what is the first thing that most people do? Join a gym and start a diet. This sounds easy enough: limit your intake of food and spend a couple of days running on a treadmill. But why is it, then, at the end of the second day, many peple are guzzling sodas, consuming chocolate, and driving three miles out of the way just to aviod the gym? It is because they are taking the outside-in approach. They start by looking for outside sources to help them lose weight. How many new diets come out each year? How many new machines promise "six-pack abs"? Most people fail because they don't realize that to lose weight, to get in shape, or to reach any kind of goal for that matter, they have to feel good about themselves, which means correcting the issues on the inside first. You have to believe you are going to do it. If this isn't the case, then no diet or exercise program is going to work.

When you tackle a goal from the inside out, then you'll increase your odds of reaching it exponentially. Let's apply the inside-out method to the previous engine light example to see the difference. Just as banging the dashboard until the red light goes off might stop the blinking but won't solve the problem, so diagnosing the interior problem and then correcting it is the right way to go. This basic principle applies to all of our goals.

The internal check up we spoke about earlier changes your frame of reference. It is impossible to solve problems externally. We at Empowered Mastery believe that any modification to a person's life, whether it is losing weight, quitting smoking, or any other major change, requires an internal commitment. Once this occurs, you begin to look at and to think about life and people differently. You will learn from future failures and not obsess over them. By accepting responsibility for the events in life, your accomplishments will increase significantly. Shifting your paradigm will only occur if you allow it to come from within.

Change your thought process ➝ Change your paradigm ➝ New positive results

{ Opinions are the cheapest commodity on earth.

—NAPOLEON HILL }

Creating a Paradigm Shift

We've just learned that what we are and what we become is a direct result of our thoughts and beliefs. You are a direct reflection of those deeply embedded beliefs that have gradually, steadily, and consistently ingrained themselves into your psyche. Our behavior is therefore informed by these beliefs, which with time become so deeply ingrained into our subconscious minds that changing them seems virtually impossible. The longer you've had your limiting beliefs, the more difficult it is to break them. To change your limiting beliefs, you will need to have different thoughts. Renewing or shifting from our current thoughts to ones that we desire brings transformation and change into our lives. This is what is known as having a paradigm shift—adopting a new way of thinking, doing things, and behaving.

66 In San Giorgi, Italy, in 1942, my dad was eleven years old. His father was in the core of engineers for the Italian army. He had to go to North Africa, serving his country in World War II. After a few months, my grandmother received the dreaded telegram that my grandfather was missing in action. Months passed, and he was presumed dead. My grandmother was raising five children with no money and no food in an impoverished small town.

About a year after my grandfather went missing, my grandmother met a gentleman she later married. In this small town there were many paradigms; one of them was 'if a widow remarries, then she is a *zoccolo*,' or, in English, a whore. The five children suffered the constant bombardment of insults from the local townspeople. As it turns out, my grandfather was a POW and returned home to his family a few years later.

The children were so happy because now they thought they could all be together again. They expected my grandmother to leave her new husband and new child and return to my grandfather. To their dismay, she couldn't do that. All five children ran away from home and lived either on the streets or in shelters. After a few years, they finally went to live with my grandfather.

I learned this truth nearly thirty-five years after I was born. While I was growing up, my dad told me that my grandmother had been killed while the American planes were bombing Italy. I kept feeling sorry for my dad. 'Imagine losing your mother to a war and dying right before your eyes.'

But that wasn't the truth at all. The story was completely fabricated by all the siblings because they held this feeling in their subconscious and couldn't find it in their hearts to forgive their mother.

All those years, and I never knew I actually had a grandmother who was alive and well. She'd been sending letters to my dad for years, but he never even opened them. Not until he received one last letter, handed to him by my own mother, who said, 'You have to go see your mother in Italy. She's dying and wants to see her children one last time.' So all the siblings got together and flew to her bedside in Italy. She was so happy that she bought ice cream for the entire hospital floor and died later that night.

The reason I am sharing this story is that our paradigms can paralyze our growth, our relationships, our spirituality, and our health. We must learn to recondition our thought process so that a tragedy like this one doesn't happen. **"**

—NICK

To replace negative, self-limiting thought patterns, you first must be aware that you have them. This is a challenging process that cannot be done overnight. It took a long time to acquire these beliefs; it will also take time to replace them with new healthy ones. Highly successful people are able to eliminate negative beliefs simply by changing their internal thought process. When you have no preconceptions limiting your progress, then you have the power to overcome temporary setbacks at the thought level. Success comes naturally when you learn how to control your thought patterns.

But how do you create a paradigm shift? How do you break down false perceptions that have been instilled and cemented into your psyche since childhood? You have to first take control of your thoughts. To achieve this paradigm shift is a great conquest. Breaking away from this mold of limited thinking begins with seven steps:

1. Improve your self-image. Voices from the inside have to be more influential then the voices on the outside. All that matters is your opinion. It's your version of the truth that matters, not theirs.
2. Stop the sabotaging self-talk. Fill your mind with encouraging words. Remove words such as "can't," "not good enough," and any other phrases that conjure negative thoughts.
3. Take responsibility. The first step in correcting a mistake is accepting its existence and your role in it. You must accept your mistakes or failures and then see yourself overcoming them!
4. Believe in yourself. You must first succeed in your mind by believing that you can do anything.
5. Change your focus. Fearful thoughts prevent you from achieving your goals. Instead of statements like, "Don't spill your drink," focus on what you want to happen and say, "Hold the cup."
6. Remain calm. When you feel overwhelmed, then you are telling your mind that it does not have the capacity to succeed.
7. Focus on the positive. Condition your mind to always view the positive components of challenges.

> The moment we want to believe something, we suddenly see all the arguments for it, and become blind to the arguments against it.
>
> —GEORGE BERNARD SHAW

POWER PARADIGMS

In the previous Success Conditioning Exercise, we asked you to replace your Paralyzing Paradigms with your new Power Paradigms. Now, we would like you to ask yourself specific questions to help generate this paradigm shift. Transfer a Paralyzing Paradigm from the previous exercise to the space below and ask yourself the following questions.

PARALYZING PARADIGM:

What will my life look like if I don't change?

Five years from now _____

Ten years from now _____

How does this make me feel? _____

How has this affected my:

Family _____

Friends _____

Coworkers _____

Transfer a Power Paradigm from the previous exercise to the space below and ask yourself the following questions.

POWER PARADIGM:

With this new Power Paradigm, how does my life look like?

Five years from now _____

Ten years from now _____

How does this make me feel? _____

How has this new belief affected my:

Family _____

Friends _____

Coworkers _____

" I had to recondition an old paradigm of mine regarding parenthood. This limiting belief was a result of a combination of experiences. Parents of the children I taught would tell me how talented I was at teaching their child, but it was always followed by 'but wait until you have your own.' My friends used to tell me my house was neat and organized, and then I heard the same old line, 'but wait until you have kids.' My wife and I have a very loving and affectionate relationship, but people would always tell us, 'You look like newlyweds now but wait until you have kids.' It may have been because I am the oldest of five children, and my father had to work very long hours so my mother could stay home with us, but I perceived this as a financial struggle. Whatever the case may be I had a fear of becoming a parent, which resulted in the Paralyzing Paradigm that children were a financial struggle and consequently would prevent me from attaining greater success in many areas of life. It wasn't until I reprogrammed my mind and created a new empowering Power Paradigm that I was able to improve my thought process. My paradigm shift helped me create my new Power Paradigm: my children are a driving force for me to consistently strive for greater success in all areas of my life. I want to show my children that their father is always willing to learn, grow, and improve. I want to be a leader for them to follow. Because of this paradigm shift, I also came to appreciate more what caring and loving parents I have. "

—PAUL

Most setbacks in life originate in our thoughts and reactions to life's issues. How we think affects how we behave and consequently the kind of actions we take—therefore, the success we attain in life is largely dependent on those actions. Most of our limitations are self-imposed and can therefore be overcome. By filling your mind with thoughts that influence positive behavior, you take positive actions and therefore achieve positive results.

Conversely, if you fill your mind with negative thoughts, then you will behave and act negatively—resulting in failure. Reprogram all the negative beliefs that prevent you from achieving success.

If you continue to do this constantly and consistently, you will, without doubt, attain gratifying success.

Don't be an emotional puppet (we will discuss this concept in Chapter 10). Don't allow any energy to be stolen by external factors. Let the past be the past, and let yesterday's results be yesterday's results. What you did yesterday produced your current results. Your future is no reflection of your past.

In Chapter 12, we will be asking you to write your Life Script. You will create a new paradigm by writing a detailed description of the new life you desire. We will be asking you to write this statement in the present tense. For now, impress the vision of your new life vividly on your mind. Pretend you are sitting in a theater and the actor and movie you are watching on screen is you and your new life. Feel the feelings, experience the joy of having it, hear the sounds and smell the scents. Add as much emotion to it as possible, as this will help it appear more realistic to your subconscious mind. Upon completion of this exercise in Chapter 12, you will find this new image soon firmly planted in your subconscious mind and ultimately expressed as reality.

> The outer conditions of a person's life will always be found to reflect their inner beliefs.
>
> —JAMES ALLEN

The X/Y Factor

The X/Y Factor describes the correlation between believing and knowing. What is the difference between the two? Belief is an expression of faith. You must have complete faith in your convictions. When you combine determination of your beliefs with the intensity of your knowledge, then there's absolutely no thread of skepticism. Look at any high-level athlete: He does not only believe that he can achieve, he knows.

This all sounds good in theory, but it's easier said than done. Let's revisit the inner workings of our mind and its relationship with the goals we want to achieve. The weight loss and exercise program we referred to earlier is a great way to demonstrate this. In Chapter 1, we talked about the two parts of the mind, the conscious and the subconscious. When making decisions, there are two other parts of your mind to consider: the X Factor and the Y Factor. Once you comprehend these factors and how they work, you will better grasp the reason why goals are sometimes difficult to achieve. This understanding will enable you to break through obstacles to your success. This X/Y Factor is one of the most powerful concepts to learn in this book. If describes perfectly the thought process we all go through on a daily basis.

Each of us suffers at some point in our lives from what we call F.A.D.: fear, anxiety, and doubt. This is the basis of the X Factor of our mind. It feeds on procrastination, and F.A.D. is the oxygen it breathes. Similar to a paradigm, the X Factor is the conditioning that resonates in our subconscious mind. A paradigm takes over your mind in a couple of ways. In many cases, you'll actually inherit this paradigm—like a certain trait—at birth. It's so firmly grounded in your family line that it becomes a genetic factor.

No matter how dated, erroneous, harmful, or wrong, these paradigms are in absolute control both of the way we think and also the decisions we make throughout our lives. But it doesn't have to be this way. For the most part, you don't know or recognize this mental conditioning until you attempt to make a major life-altering decision.

So let's closely examine how the X and Y Factor works. For example, let's say you want to quit smoking or embark on a new exercise program. This is your Y Factor, any new idea that comes to your mind. It doesn't matter what the activity is. If it's new, then your X Factor won't like it and will try to prevent this new idea from actually happening.

So when the X Factor hears that you want to get in shape, it automatically goes on alert. Some of you may recognize this as that little voice in your head describing what you can't do and why you can't do it. Every now and then, you'll talk to yourself or perhaps see people talking to themselves. Who is that? There's no one there, yet they're carrying on a conversation? This is the X Factor talking, and it's saying wait a second, hold up there on that new idea, there's no rush. Stay where you are, go back to that couch, turn on that TV and relax. Grab that remote, open up that bag of chips and have a beer. Start that exercise program next week. Your X Factor is inside your house, so to speak, and it loves being the only one there. It doesn't like to be disturbed by its eternal enemy, the Y Factor (any new idea). Does this sound familiar? Think of the last time you came up with an idea to improve or better yourself. It was an excuse as to why you couldn't succeed. That is your X Factor talking.

The Y Factor is anything that represents change, like a new idea or goal. It disrupts the status quo, and it may be the healthiest, loftiest, most wonderful idea or decision you're making in your entire life—but to your X Factor, the Y represents rebellion. The harder Y pushes for improvement, the harder X resists.

Don't misunderstand us; the desire to improve is there. Daily life can be unproductive and sabotaging no matter how much you want to improve. You are ready to shift your life into high gear. Your Y Factor wants to remove the X Factor from your mind. It's trying to cross the threshold, but your X Factor won't let it through the door.

Every time you make an explanation why this new way of life will work, your X Factor has another rational, sensible argument why it won't. So what pushes your Y Factor to the other side? Perhaps this time you don't want to stop. A desire burns deep inside. You believe you deserve it. Something inside tells you that it is yours for the taking. And so, your Y Factor pushes harder, threatening your X Factor. The minute this happens, your X Factor moves from being concerned to being afraid.

And suddenly—you're uncomfortable. Your awareness pauses and sniffs the air. In a split second, your mind has entered a new vibration—it's in upheaval. Your X Factor has given up on using your little voice—it's now decided it must stop you from embarking on that new exercise program at all costs. So it calls on its secret weapons: fear, anxiety, and doubt!

When F.A.D. enters the picture, logic leaves. When F.A.D. is a constant focus, you're only feeding the X Factor. F.A.D. trips the anxiety alarm—and nothing good can come of that. Your central nervous system goes crazy— bells and sirens go off, and the nervous chain reaction continues. All of this registers in your subconscious mind and triggers your pre-existing paradigms to not want to get in shape.

Your subconscious mind gauges the temperature or vibration your body is in. It accommodates this, which in turn produces more action in a positive or negative way. Each of us has an internal thermostat built into our subconscious minds. It is like an automatic pilot on a plane or an electronic thermostat in your home. If your house is set for seventy degrees, the electronic system automatically adjusts the heat if the room deviates from that set temperature. Your subconscious mind has been set for a certain level of success or results based on your past experiences and programming. That's why, when we back off or quit because of F.A.D., we're not telling ourselves, "Well, I'm not going to do that, because I'm afraid." Instead, we're giving ourselves a list of excuses—"Well, I'm terrible at this," or "If I try that, this will probably occur," or "It wouldn't be very good for my health because . . ." You see, every excuse our X Factor can come up with will rise to the surface—and quickly—because these paradigms have been lodged in our heads a long, long time. Excuses like I'm too tired, too old, too busy, or I'll do it next week. Or you might even try to rationalize and say, "I'm really not in such bad shape anyway."

The choice is yours. You don't have to give F.A.D. its reason to live. Make the choice to reject F.A.D. Allow yourself to become emotionally involved with what your Y Factor will do and is already doing in your life. When you focus on the Y Factor results, you're opening the door to success.

The power comes from your conscious awareness of how the mind functions and then constantly, steadfastly setting up your Y Factor to the point where it's strong enough to overpower your X Factor. Your want has to be stronger, or X will keep the door closed. And when the door does open, and Y gets in, it's got to be strong enough to stay there—it's got to be strong enough to win the battle against X and X's territory, or it will be pushed out again very quickly. This is one of the main reasons why most people go off their diets, because their Y Factor is not strong enough to push their X out.

Rationalizing keeps us in our comfort zone. You might dread going to your job every morning, and you rationalize your decision by saying "At least I have a job." Your marriage might not be much more than rote and routine. You realize that instead of truly being in love, the relationship is a habit, and rather than putting new effort into the marriage or repairing the damage, you stay where it is comfortable. This may be a familiar route. Hope fades into failure. Your X Factor remembers—and reminds you. Understand this: your X Factor cannot be trusted. It's devious and insidious. Rules don't apply, and it will win at any cost. It does not want your Y Factor to take over, and it does not want you to improve.

For every failure, for every time you settle, for everything rote in your life that's just not what you'd hoped it would be, that's your X Factor paradigm assuring you that status quo is the way to go. Who wants status quo? There is magnificence in this world—and you deserve it. You can have it. You don't want to go through life wondering, "What if?" Statements like that fill life with ifs instead of whens. Get out there and start living the life you want! Get your Y in motion! Walk up to that X Factor door of yours and break it down. And don't let that Y walk away. We don't want to say "should have," "could have," or "would have."

Remember, it doesn't take force to accomplish this. Stay calm. This state of mind gives you power over your X Factor. Don't question the state of mind—believe in it. Start with a statement, one that you truly mean. What is it—exactly—that you want and why? Write it out. Get emotionally involved with the outcome of this Y Factor in your life. How is it changing your life for the better? How are you able to change the lives of others around you because of it? Uncommonly successful people do not let their X Factor control how they think, feel, and act. They condition their Y to be stronger. Now when we say 'successful,' we are not just talking about finances. We are talking about all areas of life. Think of all the pioneers and innovators throughout history. Do you think they would let their X control them? Did they quit when faced with obstacles and challenges? Of course not. So why should you?

> 66 When I left my family business years ago, I became lazy and lethargic. For the first time in my life I stopped exercising. I was shocked to learn how easy it was for me to get into bad habits. I gained about twenty pounds. This had never happened to me before, since I always exercised, ran, or played basketball and football. However, my X Factor became so prevalent and dominant that it became my best friend. It even introduced me to its friends: my couch, the remote, the TV, and the refrigerator. So I knew I had to change things. I desperately needed to get back into shape, so I called upon my Y Factor. But before I embarked on that new exercise regime, I had to believe in myself that I could do it, otherwise it wouldn't work. That is thinking inside out and not outside in. So I decided to wake up early each morning no matter what and run three miles four days a week. Now my X Factor did not like this one bit. It gave me all the excuses in the world not to do it. It hid my sneakers and misplaced my running clothes, but I tried my best not to give in to these feelings. The first time I ran, I barely finished the three miles. The next time was difficult too. But I believed in myself and I made that committed decision so there was no turning back. Then the third time became a little easier and so did the fourth.

Before I knew it my Y Factor had not only knocked on the door but also had busted through it. As a matter of fact my Y Factor became so prevalent that it kicked my X Factor out the door itself. Now, as soon as I wake up in the morning, I have trained my subconscious mind to put on my sneakers and go for a run just as routinely as I brush my teeth and shower. My Y Factor became so dominant that it completely switched roles with my X Factor. I have so trained, conditioned, and strengthened my Y Factor that at one point I had worked out every single day for one full year. To this day, I still try to run at least five days a week, while playing basketball on weekends. I am in the best shape of my life, and I feel great! **"**

—RICK

Think of a goal you want to achieve and use the space below to complete the X/Y Factor Conditioning Exercise. Write down the reasons why you believe you can't accomplish your objective and then cross them out with an X. In the next column, write how "I can." As you write in the second column visualize every detail of what you want.

GOAL: _____

WHY I CAN'T	HOW I CAN
1.	
2.	
3.	
4.	
5.	
6.	
7.	
8.	
9.	
10.	

When you engage a Y Factor in your life, it pushes against other X Factors too. The good this brings to people's lives is unimaginable. The open door expands wider and wider for you and those around you. The more focused and the more often you write your new Y Factor affirmation, the more it permeates your subconscious mind. Most people associate the term affirmation with repetitive statements. We, however, believe these are exercises to develop your mind muscles. So in the remaining chapters, we refer to them as Mind Muscle Exercises. This practice continually impresses the Y Factor on your subconscious mind. And, little by little, it pushes out the X Factor.

Once your Y Factor becomes the norm, you'll find you're living a healthier life. However, be aware that you always have to work on your Y Factor. The weight loss scenario we used earlier is a good example of this. You've developed a healthy lifestyle, lost weight, and kept it off for a year. That's great; you've accomplished a goal, but what if you decide to compete in a marathon or triathlon? A lean body won't help you win. You have to train because you don't ever want to stop growing, do you? You must always be raising the bar if you want to continue to add to your life.

Successful people train themselves to eliminate the X factors in their mind and focus on the Y factors.

Logic dictates that if you've read this message on the X/Y Factor a couple of times, then you've understood it. But it's more than understanding we're after. We want to put a new program into our bio-hard drives. And the way to do that is by repetition. The difference between success and failure is what wins the ongoing battle in your mind between your X Factor and Y Factor. This is probably one of the most important messages you will ever hear or read, because it is truly the key to living a happier healthier life. So, step up to bat, and the next time you do something new and somebody asks you why, you'll be well equipped to let them know!

CHAPTER SUMMARY

- At a very young age, our thoughts were formed by those who were most influential in our lives.
- Paradigms and limiting beliefs control the results in your life.
- Replacing negative thoughts with productive and encouraging thoughts paves the road for improvement and success in life.
- Obstacles and setbacks in life are eliminated through a T.R.A.N.S.F.O.R.M.A.T.I.O.N. of your thought process.
- Understanding the X/Y Factor of your mind is key to achieving any goal that you set for yourself.

CHAPTER THREE

Awareness

{
Let us not look back in anger or forward in fear, but around in awareness.

—JAMES THURBER
}

In the first two chapters, we discussed the importance of your thoughts, both past and present, and how they affect your life. At times while you were reading, you may have felt uncomfortable or even a bit irritable. More often than not, looking at our past can trigger some intense emotional responses.

That's okay; it happens to everyone. As a matter of fact, by examining your thought process and releasing yourself from the prison of your past, you have taken the first step to increasing your awareness. Before we go any further, let's take a look at the seven different levels of awareness. As you read through them, see which level you are currently in.

1. Animal. This is survival mode. How do you react or respond to situations. Do you fight or flight? How are you reacting to the events in your life?

2. Mass. This level is when you let your habits and the habits of others control your life. You follow the crowd. Unfortunately, the crowd doesn't have your best interests in mind. As you travel with the crowd, you are caught up in what they think of you.

3. (Terror Barrier) Understanding. You start to realize that you want something more in your life. Something is missing. At this level, you examine your paradigms and question who you are. Through this questioning, you become a stronger person. You desire to be, to do, or to have more. At this level, you have a propensity to act but don't because you're too concerned with what others may think of you.

4. Individual. At this level, you begin to understand your unique abilities and create a desire to express them.

5. Discipline. This is the level that separates you from the pack. You begin to express your own unique qualities. You are able to formulate a plan and see it through regardless of the circumstances.

6. Recondition. Through experience, you learn. As you engage in learning about yourself, you become emotionally involved and form a connection. Once this happens, change is inevitable. As you travel through this level, your self-discipline increases, empowering you to learn more, to experience more, and ultimately to attain the seventh level.

7. Dissociation. The physical world no longer controls you. At this level, you gain self-control and your thoughts guide you through your world. This is the highest level of awareness attainable. Once you have achieved this level, you have achieved freedom.

What level of awareness are you currently in? How can you elevate to a higher level? In order to gain a new perspective on life, you must first challenge your current one. This is like taking two steps backward before being able to take one step forward. This enables you to look deep inside yourself and stop traveling through life as if you are on an assembly line. Once you gain this understanding, you can find out who you truly are and where you really want to go and can stop living through other people's expectations about how you should live your life. Breaking free of your false self and finding the true you brings a sense of empowerment. You can start to make conscious decisions to turn your wants into reality.

66 My level of awareness is at its peak when I am teaching a martial arts class or speaking at our seminars. I can actually see all of my surroundings, including students and their parents. I am able to scan around and notice if a student has not been in class in a while, if it's someone's first class, if my staff is doing a good job teaching their group, if parents in the waiting area are paying attention or talking amongst themselves. I sense the level of energy in the room. I am even able to sense the positive or negative energy of those around me. My five senses of sight, touch, taste, smell and hearing are at their apex. 99

—PAUL

In the space below, reflect on your life and describe two times when your level of awareness was at its peak and why.

1.

2.

Stress and tension drain the mind of all productive energy. In today's society, there is a tremendous amount of pressure, perhaps more than ever before. We live in a competitive, cutthroat age. Too many worries in life throw you into a vicious cycle in which negative thoughts take over and become the focus of attention. Once this happens, you've lost the ability to tap into a higher state of awareness.

Connecting to this higher state of awareness is relatively simple. Stay calm. This allows you to control your thoughts more effectively. In Chapter 9, we teach you a few simple breathing techniques and meditation methods to achieve and maintain a state of calmness. Have you ever noticed how people who are calm and collected seem to be that way all of the time? Think back to a time when a problem came up; how did you react? Did you panic, or were you in a state of calmness? Did your reaction make the situation better or worse? Remember Rick's story in Chapter 1 where he was agitated over a projector? Rick was unable to be productive, while Chris and Paul stayed calm and were able to focus on the task at hand.

Learning to relax and freeing your mind of unwanted tension is critical for eliminating the events and circumstances that control you. Watch for signs of upcoming stress and look for alternatives or solutions that offset the pressure. Once you are able to relax, you create a balance in life that enables a sense of confidence and composure, hence increasing your level of awareness This results in you being able to accomplish your daily tasks in a smooth and efficient manner.

Awareness is a key element in martial arts training. A heightened level of awareness gives anyone the edge in training and real life situations. Victims are not randomly chosen. They are typically chosen due to their distractibility and cluelessness of their surroundings. Now, there is a difference between having awareness and being obsessive about it. Being at a higher level of awareness lets you see your surroundings with a kind of peripheral shield around you, recognizing any situations of concern. Being overly concerned or scared about being a victim will give you more stress and anxiety ultimately causing you to freeze up in a situation.

> When every physical and mental resource is focused,
> one's power to solve a problem multiplies tremendously.
>
> —NORMAN VINCENT PEALE

What is Your IQ?

Most of us are born with five senses that help us to perceive what we see, taste, touch, hear, and smell. By the age of five, most of us have good comprehension of our five senses' abilities to understand the world and the environment around us. However, the five senses are limited to just telling and showing us what already "is." They have no power to create or transform.

In order to create or transform, you must expand your mind beyond your normal capabilities and use the intellectual qualities (IQ) referred to in Chapter 1. These intellectual qualities are present in everyone and have the power to create and transform. Each intellectual quality identifies a powerful area of thought that can be used to transform our lives. More importantly, we are all born with the ability to develop and strengthen these innate abilities.

As previously mentioned, the intellectual qualities are:

- Imagination
- Confidence
- Optimism
- Desire (Burning)
- Passion
- Commitment
- Faith
- Vision
- Living through your Worthy Ideal

Each of us was placed here for a specific reason. Over time, our IQ evolves to better enable us to fulfill our purpose. Through the use of our IQ, we can achieve a higher level of thinking and decision-making, which results in extraordinary success. These are our mind muscles and just like our physical muscles, they must be exercised. They may be weak or strong depending on how much they are used. Let's compare these mind muscles to the physical muscles in your body. If you exercise your muscles in a healthy manner, they will grow and expand, but the moment you stop, they shrink and weaken. Our IQ operates in the same way. For us to utilize our mind and provide each of us with infinite power and inner strength, we must develop these qualities and come to the realization that these qualities are always at work. The majority of successful people have cultivated these qualities. Their successes offer us clues for our own betterment. Because each IQ is so important, we want to take a moment and discuss them separately. To help, we've included Conditioning Exercises at the end of each IQ.

Imagination

What separates us from every living creature on this universe? Our ability to imagine. Everything that was invented was at first someone's imagination. The definition of imagination is the act or power of forming a mental image of something not present to the senses or never before wholly perceived in reality.

As mentioned at the start, everything starts with a thought, this requires us to imagine. As we get older we lose the ability to imagine. We are now giving you permission to be a kid again.

EXERCISE:

List 3 instances where you used our IQ of Imagination for something positive.

1.

2.

3.

More about Imagination in Chapter 12.

Confidence

Have you ever been on a sales call or presenting during a meeting where you just knew you would do well? Or went into an exam or test at school and knew you would ace it? Weren't those great feelings? You had that inner confidence where you just knew things would go well. Wouldn't it be great to feel that way all the time? All successful people in life have attained a level of confidence in all areas of their lives; confidence in their work abilities, confidence in their relationships, confidence in their financial future.

Some of us seem to be born with this IQ, others develop it over time. Either way we need to work at it. Confidence is the difference between belief and knowing. You can believe you can achieve something, but not actually do so. When you know you will achieve something you have that innermost confidence that it will happen.

> 66 We were playing in a national college flag football tournament in New Orleans. Adelphi U. was a division III small private college with no regular football team. Through the luck of the draw we found ourselves playing against the University of Arkansas in our opening game. At first our whole team thought there was no way we could beat this huge division I school. Their flag football team was probably as good as most division II regular football teams whereas most of our team didn't even play high school football. We walked out on that field to warm up and for some reason we developed this confidence that somehow we were going to win. We didn't just believe we could but KNEW we would. It was an incredible feeling where we just knew the outcome. We pulled away in the 2nd half and ended up winning by a wide margin. We still to this day talk about that game. 99
>
> **NICK & RICK**

Exercise: List 5 instances where you were confident of the outcome of your actions.

1.

2.

3.

4.

5.

{ A pessimist sees the difficulty in every opportunity; an
optimist sees the opportunity in every difficulty.

—WINSTON CHURCHILL }

Optimism

Everyone is an optimist when things are going their way. But what about
when things aren't so good? You have the ability to see the good in all aspects
of your life. However, without optimism, you feel hopeless. Once you fall into
a state of hopelessness, you no longer have the courage to continue searching
for solutions. Instead, you are stuck in the disaster mindset. You might have
heard of the Law of Attraction, which states that like attracts like. If you
are optimistic, most likely you will attract optimistic people, events and
circumstances into your life. It brings about the needed change to create a
better world.

In life, we experience both successes and failures. Focusing on the
positives (even if there is only one out of a hundred) will realign your thoughts
and soon, through the Law of Attraction, the negatives are eliminated and
replaced with good and beneficial items. Remember, the opposite is true as
well. Optimism is about training yourself to become a good finder. You can
program your subconscious mind to search for the good in any person, situation,
or event. How? First you must be aware of the questions you are asking. By
consciously asking yourself positive questions, you help train your subconscious
to think in the positive. What is good about this person? What am I appreciative
for in my life? What can I learn from this situation? Your mind will search for
answers to whatever questions you are asking yourself.

Give yourself the gift of positive focus. We begin all our coaching sessions
for schools, corporations, and individuals with this one question—what went
well this week? This begins to train your mind to be a good finder and to
search for the good in your life. This is not an easy exercise, but when you
begin to ask yourself the right questions, then you will open your mind to a
new world of possibilities. This is agreat exercise to do with your kids during
dinner.

Do you view situations as a problem or a challenge? What if you begin thinking of your challenges as opportunities? One portion of the seminars and workshops that we do with corporations is called the C.O.S., which stands for Challenge, Opportunities, and Strengths exercise. We ask three powerful questions:

1. What are some challenges your company may be facing with staff, customers, or business?
2. What opportunities do you have by participating in our coaching process?
3. What strengths does your company currently have that you want us to help improve over the next quarter?

We then begin to ask a series of questions that lead to solutions for their current challenges.

Optimism must be developed and nurtured in our minds. By doing so, we encourage ourselves not only to create a better life for us but also to act as an example for someone who is the eternal pessimist. Optimism is contagious. It brings about the needed change to create a better world.

66 We train our staff to become good finders when teaching our students. If a student is doing something wrong, we never just walk up and correct them. We catch them doing something right and then point out the previous mistake. After we correct the student, we then praise the correction. We call this Praise-Correct-Praise. By applying this technique, we consistently search for the good in all our students. So if a child is wiggling around we will say, 'Wow, you have such awesome energy today, now let me see how you show self-control like a black belt.' When the child sits straight up, then we say, 'Great job! Now you look like a leader who demonstrates self-control.' 99

—PAUL & CHRIS

LIST TEN THINGS THAT WENT WELL THIS WEEK.

1.

2.

3.

4.

5.

6.

7.

8.

9.

10.

> It is for us to pray not for tasks equal to our powers, but for powers equal to our tasks, to go forward with a great desire forever beating at the door of our hearts as we travel toward our distant goal.
>
> —HELEN KELLER

Desire

Desire is a powerful force for attracting what you want. Everything you create begins with desire. Desire your dreams so much that you convince yourself that you have them now. See and feel and believe that you're already living your dream. The moment your desire becomes belief, then you have transformed your mind into a state of creation.

How excited are you about manifesting your desires? When you want something so much that you can feel it, when you're thrilled, excited, and eager with anticipation, when it feels so real that you can taste it, you have a strong burning desire. You can also tell by the way you feel if you're allowing or resisting. When you focus on your desire and feel good, you're allowing. When you focus on your desire and feel bad, you're resisting.

With a strong, burning desire, you are letting go of resistance and consciously empowering your dreams to become reality.

66 At 28, my father became totally blind (I was two years old). He could have simply given in to his handicap, but he had an unstoppable, burning desire to overcome this obstacle in order to succeed and provide for his family. Through urging and support from my mother, he left his current job and opened his own textile business, despite knowing that the industry was all about 'seeing' color and patterns. He never once gave in to his blindness, refusing even a cane or a Seeing Eye dog. We lived in the suburbs of New York, and my mother would take him back and forth from the train each day for his commute into Manhattan. He made friends with

fellow riders, who would save a seat for him, and he rarely had to show his ticket, as all the conductors knew him. He had coworkers who would take him back and forth from the train to work. Failure was never an option, and his success as a businessman and as a human being was an incredible testament to his burning desire to overcome and succeed despite his lack of sight. **99**

—RICK

WHAT THREE ITEMS DO YOU DESIRE MORE THAN ANYTHING ELSE IN THE WORLD?

1.

2.

3.

Passion

> Passion is the element in which we live; without it, we hardly vegetate.
>
> —LORD BYRON

What is the difference between passion and purpose? We often hear this question in our seminars. Passion is a powerful emotion. It is an unstoppable enthusiasm to succeed in anything you do, while purpose is something you constantly strive toward. (Purpose is detailed further in Chapter 8.) While the question above is valid, more appropriately we should ask, "What does it mean to have passion?" What separates people with it and without it? Success and fulfillment is the differentiating factor.

How passionate are you about living your dreams? Passion is one of life's most powerful forces. It's the fuel that propels you forward against all odds and obstacles, enabling you to conquer your circumstances. This particular intellectual quality takes you through life's highs and lows and enables you to be more expressive, articulate, and adventurous. You are more apt to embark on a journey of creation. Combining passion with devotion and dedication creates the vision to see anything you desire come to fruition.

With passion, you can defy any obstacle aggressively, grow progressively, and live purposefully.

LIST TEN THINGS THAT YOU ARE PASSIONATE ABOUT

1.

2.

3.

4.

5.

6.

7.

8.

9.

10.

> The quality of a person's life is in direct proportion to their commitment to excellence, regardless of their chosen field of endeavor.
>
> —VINCE LOMBARDI

Commitment

Commitment gives us the courage to persevere despite all obstacles. When committed, you will do whatever it takes to achieve that result. It is a force of your mind that becomes evident and that will not take no for an answer. Recalling the X/Y Factor, commitment is the X Factor's kryptonite. Commitment pushes beyond the resistance in your mind that says you can't do something and finds a way to do it and to do it well. In doing this, you also push yourself physically beyond your comfort level to new heights of success. In your mind, you've vowed to reach your goal and don't stop until you do. Many people have achieved great results, and you will too. A firm commitment powers great successes and great rewards.

This dedication is the force of will to do all the little details just as well as the big ones. It enables you to move through and find a way when nothing seems to work. It is trying everything and then adding new ideas to get the results you want. You are constantly focused on how to achieve the results you have set your sights on.

Commitment helps reach the next level through the steps of learning, growing, and building—one step at a time and one process at a time. You tap into a strong place deep inside to go forward, even when faced with exhaustion, frustration, or a dead end. Once this occurs, your strength is resolved.

Anything is possible with Commitment.

" My brother had set a goal to swim the English Channel. He was always a good swimmer and competed in triathlons but never swam more than a couple of miles. The English Channel is known as the Everest of open water swims. It's approximately nineteen miles, and due to the ever changing tides and weather conditions, the success rate is less than 50 percent.

Notwithstanding those obstacles, my brother also had to find the time to train while working fifty to sixty hours per week. He made a commitment to wake up at 4:30 every morning to train. After work, he trained again for at least an hour. Every weekend, no matter the weather, he swam in the open waters of the Long Island Sound or, when possible, the Atlantic Ocean. If the natural obstacles of distance and the nature of the English Channel weren't enough to deter someone, there were also specific guidelines for the swim, like not being allowed to wear a wet suit. The most demanding and cruelest rule was that during the whole time in the water you were not allowed to even touch the boat that follows you without being disqualified. Despite all of this, my brother, through dedicated commitment, passion, and burning desire, successfully swam the English Channel. As of this writing fewer than 3,000 in history have ever accomplished this feat. "

—RICK

LIST 7 TIMES WHERE YOU PUSHED YOURSELF FURTHER THAN YOU THOUGHT POSSIBLE

1.

2.

3.

4.

5.

6.

7.

FAITH

Faith is defined as something that is believed with strong conviction; especially a system of religious beliefs. Now we are extremely respectful and aware of everyone's religion and religious beliefs. So as we say in our coaching programs and seminars, two things we will not talk about are religion and politics. The same holds true for this book.

We believe that everyone should have faith in something; whether it is to a higher power, religion, or simply faith in your loved ones.

But faith can also be used as a powerful tool to accomplish, achieve and improve your life.

The power of faith gives you the perspective you need to observe and accept the unpredictable future and avoid getting lost when self-doubt surfaces.

Faith is a choice informed by careful self-examination and an assessment of who you really are and what you are capable of. Successful people are driven by their unshakeable faith in what they are trying to accomplish. It is the power of their faith that minimizes the risk in any endeavor.

They have a strong faith in themselves, which enables them to weather what others would consider to be catastrophic failures. They don't stop until they find success. No stumbling block or obstacle curbs their faith. Making conscious choices means having faith that you can exert the effort required to succeed in any given venture. Use the power of your faith to focus yourself on the success you deserve.

66 In 1993, my wife and I lost a child. We then decided to undergo IVF. Three eggs were implanted, and the day before Thanksgiving, my wife started to bleed. The doctor couldn't see us until Friday morning. He told us that she'd likely miscarried and that we should plan on a D & C. As we were waiting in the doctor's office for the sonogram, my wife asked me, 'Do you believe in miracles?' With the death of my first child and now this, I had a difficult time believing anything, so I said, 'No.' She told me I should always have hope and faith. The doctor came in and turned the monitor away before he began the sonogram. During the procedure, he suddenly yelled to his nurse, 'Mary get in here!' He turned the monitor toward us and asked, 'Do you believe in miracles?' We saw what is now our son. The other eggs had miscarried. I've never stopped believing since. **99**

—NICK

LIST 10 THINGS YOU BELIEVE AND HAVE FAITH IN

1.

2.

3.

4.

5.

6.

7.

8.

9.

10.

{
Vision is the art of seeing things invisible.

—JONATHAN SWIFT
}

Vision

Do you have a vision for your life? All successful people have a clear, solid vision. It is a very powerful intellectual quality to nurture, because when it gets strong enough, then nothing can stop you from achieving what you set out to do. If you want to become successful, it's very important to have a strong vision. One of the most important aspects of a vision is the strength it provides to keep on pressing for success in the midst of every opposition. You'll face all kinds of challenges that will serve to discourage you, but if you have a strong enough vision, then you won't let anything stop you.

Vision also has the power to attract other people that will help you fulfill it. People follow others who have a strong conviction. Vision brings people to you who wouldn't ordinarily be attracted to you. Just think about some of the most successful people in your life. Most probably have such conviction about what they do that when they talk to you, it makes you want to help them any way you can.

Develop a vision for your life. Once you have, you'll experience what the power of a vision can do for you. Don't be afraid to let it be a big vision either. You have more in you than you could possibly know. Your vision has the potential to change millions of lives around the world.

> **❝** One of my lifelong visions was to test for a black belt degree in Korea. Another vision was to do this with my younger brother. Because I'd trained in martial arts even before he was born, we never really had time between each rank to test side by side. In 1999, I had the opportunity to test for my fifth degree black belt in Korea but unfortunately had to have a hernia operation two weeks prior to leaving. In 2001, my brother had the opportunity to test for his fourth degree black belt in Korea. All the while, I held a strong vision of testing for this higher level with him on the screen of my mind. In the beginning of 2008, our grand master asked us both to travel to Korea to test for our fifth and sixth degree black belts along with three of my martial arts best friends. What made it even more special was that my father came along with us to watch us both graduate. The vision of both of us testing in Korea and the chance to share this opportunity with my brother, training partners, and my father was a dream come true. **❞**
>
> —PAUL

> 66 In July of 2008, I had the opportunity to go with my son and my dad to Korea with my mentor Paul Melella and the Taekwondo school to compete in an international competition. We were riding on the bus on the way to the stadium. I sat next to Paul on the bus (in martial arts, he is better known as Master Melella). I was worried and a bit scared, because I hadn't trained as hard as I should have. I said to Paul, 'Maybe I shouldn't compete. I may not be ready.' He replied, 'Visualize victory, practice what you preach.' I began to visualize victory and suddenly that burning desire began to take over to win. Needless to say, I won the silver medal in the international sparring and forms competition. 99
>
> —NICK

WHAT IS YOUR VISION, PROFESSIONALLY, PERSONALLY, FINANCIALLY?

Professional Vision

Personal Vision

Financial Vision

> A new way of thinking has become the necessary condition for responsible living and acting. If we maintain obsolete values and beliefs, a fragmented consciousness and a self-centered spirit, we will continue to hold on to outdated goals and behaviors.
>
> —DALAI LAMA

Living Through Your Worthy Ideal

The last of Empowered Mastery's IQ's is what truly makes us and will make you UNCOMMON. All the previous IQ's are necessary ingredients that make up your Worthy Ideal.

You are about to learn the foundation of Empowered Mastery's coaching program. It is WHY we do what we do! This is what separates us from 95% of the other coaching programs. It is this concept that makes us UNCOMMON. When you understand and discover your Worthy Ideal, everything around you changes. Your level of awareness increases exponentially.

AWARENESS GIVES MEANING TO LIFE

The awareness you are seeking requires replacing old conditioning; conditioning which is genetic and environmental. This is a lifelong process for nearly every living person. Conditioning is a multitude of ideas which are fixed in your subconscious mind. Fixed ideas are more commonly referred to as habits. You have a host of concepts fixed in your subconscious mind which require replacing. They are causing the unwanted results you are currently getting. These ideas are holding you back, stifling your growth. They are negative and therefore destructive. Negative habits, if broken and not consciously replaced with positive habits, will be replaced almost immediately by other negative habits. Nature abhors a vacuum. To be successful in replacing negative habits with positive ones, you must have a good reason.

That good reason is a **Worthy Ideal!**

Have you ever set a goal and not attained it? Why do most people never achieve their goals in life? Did you ever achieve a goal and then say to yourself "Is that it?" Why is that?

Well, we believe the reason people don't achieve their goals is because they are not aligned with what we call a Worthy Ideal. Goals are really just a by-product of a Worthy Ideal. A Worthy Ideal is what we like to call the "Big Picture" of your life. And it is the driving force to all the goals that you want to achieve. Goals come and go but a Worthy Ideal is forever. Goals are destinations, your Worthy Ideal is your lifelong journey.

Your Worthy Ideal should be so exciting, so powerful, so exhilarating, that you would be willing to give your life for it. It combines an idea or image with an intense desire and passion. As you develop your Worthy Ideal, you'll find that it will be driven by an unrelenting force.

It inspires you to continue and persist regardless of your surroundings.

When you live this way your life reaches a level of fulfillment unsurpassed by anything you have ever experienced. Most people confuse a Worthy Ideal with a goal. An objective or goal is relatively common, like a new car, a new home, or reaching a sales target at work. Once accomplished, you move on to the next one. (Chapter 11 specifically deals with targeting goals.) A goal lacks the prestige and significance of a Worthy Ideal.

The best example of what a Worthy Ideal is and how powerful and impacting it can be, is the following quote:

> "I have dedicated myself to this struggle of the African people. I have fought against white domination and I fought against black domination. I have cherished the [worthy] Ideal of a democratic and free society in which all persons live together in harmony with equal opportunities. It is a [Worthy] [I]deal I hope to live for and to achieve. But my lord, if needs be it is a [Worthy] Ideal, for which I am prepared to die."
>
> – NELSON MANDELA, FROM HIS SPEECH AT HIS TRIAL IN 1964 AND REPEATED WHEN HE WAS RELEASED FROM PRISON IN CAPE TOWN, 11 FEBRUARY 1990.

Here are other examples of Worthy Ideals:

Martin Luther King Jr. – non violent protest

Bill Gates – Productivity and achievement of potential

Steve Jobs – Challenging the status quo and empowering the individual

Gloria Stienem – Women's liberation

REMEMBER: A WORTHY IDEAL is so much more powerful than a goal. All successful (uncommon) people throughout history had a WORTHY IDEAL that drove them.

Your Worthy Ideal is your "Big Picture" and should also be bigger than you. If you really think about it, your Worthy Ideal drives almost every action you make and every goal you set. Any action steps that you take and most of your personal goals are really just a by-product of your Worthy Ideal. Our signature programs, the T.R.A.N.S.F.O.R.M.A.T.I.O.N. Doctrine, and this book, *YOU Have Infinite Power*, are just by-products or goals that are aligned with our Worthy Ideal. That's really why most people don't accomplish their goals—because their goals may not be aligned with their Worthy Ideal; or some people may not consciously know what their Worthy Ideal is.

Your Worthy Ideal is effortless, fun, and exhilarating. You don't consider it work; it excites you twenty-four hours a day, 365 days a year.

You will know when you have discovered your Worthy Ideal when:

1. You are inspired to accomplish any feat that you once thought impossible.

2. You are so driven by passion, emotion, and burning desire, that nothing will stop you from reaching your goals.

3. You feel your Worthy Ideal in the pit of your stomach. It is a gut instinct.

4. Your level of awareness rises at the mere thought of your Worthy Ideal, and you begin to feel an inner strength.

5. You've discovered your Worthy Ideal when work becomes fun.

6. Your Worthy Ideal is bigger than you. It's more than who you become, what you do, or what you achieve.

We believe every single one of us has a Worthy Ideal to fulfill. Through our experience, we believe it is hardwired into us and we either have the awareness to recognize it or we don't.

One of the first things we suggest you do in our Worthy Ideal concept is to begin to reflect upon your childhood or on certain things, events, situations or people throughout your life that have moved you.

Next, pay attention to the things that felt like you were really "on," when you were doing something—a task where it didn't matter how much time you took or whether you got paid or not! You could do it for hours and still have the energy to do it. Have you ever imagined or planned something that kept you up all night? An idea or thought that just unleashed an energy or passion? The reason you felt this way, was because you were tapped into your Worthy Ideal.

EXERCISE:

Reflect upon your childhood or certain things, events situations and/ or people throughout your life that have inspired you. Things you did when you felt exhilarated. Then simply start writing.

ff I had a childhood bully who was my neighbor, lived on my block, was in my class, and rode my school bus. Everywhere I went, he was there. It was like I couldn't avoid him. He beat me up almost every day. One day, my mother enrolled me into martial arts. I secretly trained for about six months and my bully tried to pick on me. Because of my martial arts training I had developed the confidence to stand up to him. I actually kicked him in the nose and made him bleed. After that day, he never picked on me again. Ironically we became childhood best friends and I was the best man at his wedding.

That experience inspired me to begin teaching children that were small, not confident, or easy targets for bullies. I remember how my life was impacted through martial arts and I am driven to help them develop a confident self image to help them succeed in life.

Then my Worthy Ideal evolved into training students to become great fighters and competitive martial arts athletes. I traveled around the world taking my tournament team to competitions. I coached students to become national champions in sparring, but not in life. I was witnessing some of my students that were great fighters get into trouble and some into the wrong crowds.

I then watched a movie called *The Karate Kid* (the original). Do you remember the movie? In this movie there were two different kinds of instructors. One was the Sensei from the Kobra Kai Dojo which only taught kids how to fight and win tournaments...the other was Mr. Miagi, who taught not only martial arts, but also lessons about life.

So after watching this movie, my Worthy Ideal evolved once more, this time into teaching children about character development and becoming good people.

Because I was making a more positive impact, parents began joining my classes, and I shifted my Worthy Ideal to not only teach martial arts, and character development, but to empasize spending quality time as a family. The parents I had as students began to lose weight and feel better about themselves. I said to myself, wow, I am impacting more people —not just children, but entire families.

I wanted to help more people improve not just physically but in all areas of life. I traveled around the world and studied some of the best trainers that taught human potential. Every book, audio program and seminar that I could get my hands on I read, listened, and attended. It totally transformed my personal and business life. I then began implementing the personal development technology that I was studying into my classes. My adult clients began coming back to me and sharing how they were receiving job promotions and opening up their own business because of what I was teaching them. I said to myself, 'wow if only I could impact more people!' So that's how Empowered Mastery was formed. There were only a certain amount of people I could impact within the community in which I was teaching martial arts. But now, my partners and I are impacting corporations, schools, and people all over the world with the TRANSFORMATION Doctrine.

Now, My Worthy Ideal is to lead, teach and inspire children, families and business professionals to reach their personal full potential in all areas of life. Physically, mentally, emotionally, spiritually, and professionally,so that they can achieve ultimate success and live a healthy, vital life of happiness and fulfillment. **"**

-PAUL

The Worthy Ideal concept is the most challenging area of the T.R.A.N.S.F.O.R.M.A.T.I.O.N. Doctrine for some people to grasp. But, once you are aware of and define your Worthy Ideal, it's like punching in an address into a GPS. You know that driving to your destinations in life will be a piece of cake because you will be guided along the way. Now, you may be saying, "Isn't the GPS example a destination?" The answer is yes it is. Your Worthy Ideal typically won't be the final "destination" but a never-ending journey. But if you don't KNOW what direction you want to go, then you will just be someone getting into a car and driving around. Remember, as you drive in this journey of life, each destination (goal) is a small rest stop or target that you want to hit along the way.

When you are aware of your Worthy Ideal the journey of life becomes enjoyable and any fear, anxiety and doubt of driving around for no apparent reason is eliminated. The purpose of the drive has meaning and you have an idea of what direction you are traveling, know how you are getting there, and why are you are driving.

All of our previously mentioned IQ's are words we use to describe our human need to identify the awareness of our Worthy Ideal. Ultimately, realizing this Worthy Ideal is a spiritual quest. It represents your ability to connect with something greater than yourself. Isn't that what we all want to do—make a difference in the lives of others and leave a legacy when we're gone? That's why we formed Empowered Mastery. Though all four of us were successful in our own rights, there was still something missing. We want to inspire people across the world to lead a life of fulfillment. In turn, they will want to do the same for others.

Becoming aware of a Worthy Ideal must be compelling. It creates an inner sense of urgency and allows you to feel alive and invigorated.

What makes you feel alive and invigorated?

Your Worthy Ideal should stimulate and energize you. It describes you perfectly. Sometimes your actual life or work turns out to be completely different from your purpose. It just doesn't match. This is a good indicator that you have been living a life out of alignment with your Worthy Ideal. In essence, you've not living according to your Worthy Ideal.

How many people dislike what they do for a living? How many people work 40 hours a week, commuting hours a day to a job they can't wait to leave? We can venture to say that most of these people have not discovered and are not living through their Worthy Ideal.

> 66 I worked in NYC for 15 years, commuting 3 hours a day to a job I ended up hating. I watched the clock and couldn't wait until it was time to leave. I hardly saw my kids during the week. I was miserable.
>
> It wasn't until joining with my partners and forming Empowered Mastery that I rediscovered my passion. It took me 47 years to discover my Worthy Ideal. I no longer watch the clock as I truly love what I do. That is the power of living through one's Worthy Ideal. 99
>
> -RICK

If this is true in your own life, then awareness is your starting point. You might want to start planning a new, more fitting and rewarding life, career, or both. As we stated earlier, your Worthy Ideal should be your legacy—it's larger than you. It should be an ongoing quest, so that when you're ready to leave this life, you know you've impacted other people in a positive way.

Remember—tomorrow is the first day of the rest of your life.

Empowered Mastery's Worthy Ideal *is to inspire and impact professionals and entrepreneurs to achieve ULTIMATE success Personally, Professionally, Spiritually, and Physically so they can live a life filled with passion and purpose.*

WORTHY IDEAL COMPONENTS

Here is a template to follow to help you create your Worthy Ideal. Your Worthy Ideal can be geared toward your personal life, your career or preferably both. Use our Worthy Ideal above as a guide.

To _____ and _____
(Use a powerful action verb or verbs that resonate with you)

_____ and _____
(State your Ideal Clients and/or specific people or groups of people)

To _____
_____
_____
(To do what? What is your burning desire to do for them?)

So they can _____
_____
_____
(What is the benefit and value your burning desire provides?)

NOTE: Make sure the words you choose resonate not only with you but your Ideal Clients/groups as well.

The Worthy Ideal concept is the beginning of a process we call, The L.A.B report. It stands for "LIFE ALIGNMENT BLUEPRINT." A house needs a blueprint in order to be built. If it doesn't have the correct blueprint, the house may not be built correctly. The same rule applies with life. Designing your personalized Life Blueprint will assist you to live a more fulfilling and balanced life filled with passion and purpose. It will help you establish a clear vision to accomplish your goals.

The L.A.B Report is a combination of four letters in our T.R.A.N.S.F.O.R.M.A.T.I.O.N Doctrine.

Awareness—Which will assist you to create your Worthy Ideal.
Realization—Which will assist you to create your Life's Purpose.
Focus—Which will assist you to create your Core Four Areas of Life.
Track your goals—Which will assist you to align your goals with your Worthy Ideal, Life's Purpose and top Areas of Life.

EMC'S L.A.B. REPORT

The Worthy Ideal (why you do what you do) leads you toward your Life's Purpose (how you will do it), which will lead you to the top important areas of your life and then all of your goals will be in alignment with your Worthy Ideal.

At Empowered Mastery we are able to take our Worthy Ideal to a higher level by teaching our T.R.A.N.S.F.O.R.M.A.T.I.O.N. Doctrine to all our clients. Our Worthy Ideal not only helps the lives of our students, it also improves the mindset and belief system of our family and generations after us. Most of all, it helps us personally. We are all far from perfect, but by teaching our process, it helps us continuously condition our conscious and subconscious minds.

We'd like to take this opportunity to share with you how our Worthy Ideals were created.

66 When I decided to become a martial arts professional, people questioned me as to why. I was told to find a real job and teach part-time after work, that you can't make a living teaching martial arts. I remember that I didn't care what others thought. I love what I do, because I make a difference in other people's lives. I had a vision to own one of the most successful martial arts schools in the country, maybe to prove others wrong or prove to myself that I can do it. Either way, my Worthy Ideal was to use martial arts as a vehicle to impact and develop good people by teaching positive life skills and values. So I sought out one of my students at the time. He was my Master in the world of finances. It turned out this person shared my passion and desire to inspire as many people as he could to lead a financially secure and healthy life. What was ironic is he was limited in his impact to just his clients. I told him about an opportunity to train under Bob Proctor who was running a school in Florida. As you might have guessed the person I am referring to is my partner Nick. The rest as we say is history. Now, with the creation of Empowered Mastery, my partners and I are able to impact thousands of people in this country as well as millions of people around the world. 99

—PAUL

66 I was successful in all of my past business endeavors. I retired at the age of 39. Yet something was missing. I had more money than I needed. I had the luxury of free time that most people don't get until they are too old to enjoy it. People envied my life, yet I was miserable. I had no focus, no passion, and no burning desire. I learned the hard way that money does not buy happiness and money does not mean you are successful. What I lacked was a Worthy Ideal. Now with the creation of our company, Empowered Mastery, I wake up in the morning feeling more energized than I've felt in my entire life. I truly love what I do. I no longer have a job or even a career. I have something infinitely more powerful; a

LIFESTYLE! I have learned first hand when you discover your Worthy Ideal, everything around you changes for the better. "

—RICK

" In my martial arts academy, I teach people of all ages, backgrounds, and abilities. I remember when I opened my academy; I questioned whether or not I should have pursued a teaching career. Looking back on that time in my life, I am extremely happy and grateful that I went in the direction I did. I remember talking to Paul and asking him whether or not I should do it. He said to me, 'This is you; you are a professional martial artist. You have to do it.' I also remember thinking that, as a teacher, I would get financial security, summers off, and be home to eat dinner with my children. I also remember thinking that being a martial arts school owner meant that the success of the school was solely dependent on me. I now realize that thought came only out of fear. With Paul's help, I realized that through martial arts I could impact and create a better society for all people in the community; not just the twenty-five kids I would have had in a classroom. I also get to see students grow from young children to confident, strong adults, who make a positive contribution to society. No career is more rewarding than that. "

—CHRIS

" When I was growing up, my father always told me to become a doctor or a lawyer. After college when I decided to go into financial services, my dad said to me, 'It's ok, until you go to medical or law school. Then you'll have a real career.' After a few years of working in financial services, I realized that I was impacting lives. My clients were appreciative for the wealth and legacy I helped create. I began to feel great about the impact that I made in their lives.

As a financial advisor I helped thousands obtain a better quality of life. Now, through Empowered Mastery, I am able to teach people outside the financial services arena how to tap into the power of the mind in order to live a life of passion and purpose. By doing so, I can begin the process of changing people and society to make the world a better place for future generations. This is the legacy that I plan on leaving behind. **"**

—NICK

WHAT IS YOUR WORTHY IDEAL? WHEN ANSWERING THIS QUESTION, DON'T THINK OF "HOW I CAN" OR "WHY I CAN'T." JUST LET YOUR IMAGINATION FLOW AND WRITE WHAT COMES TO YOUR MIND FIRST.

CHAPTER SUMMARY

- The level of awareness you are currently living in dictates your current status in life.
- Everyone is born with the same IQ to succeed in life.
- Stress and tension prevent you from attaining a high state of awareness.
- Discovering and living through your Worthy Ideal is what separates the UNCOMMON from the common, the successful from the status quo.
- You need to think beyond your five senses and use your intellectual qualities.

CHAPTER FOUR

Never Give Up

{
Many of life's failures are people who did not realize how close they were to success when they gave up.

—THOMAS EDISON
}

Persistence is one of the most crucial elements in attaining success in any endeavor. It is a combination of two key elements: will and desire. Partnering these two elements enables you to achieve great accomplishments. Persistence gives you the power to overcome all obstacles and setbacks that come along as you are on your path to living through your Worthy Ideal.

Thomas Edison is the classic example of a person who exemplifies persistence. It took him ten thousand tries to finally succeed in inventing the light bulb. Talk about will and desire! One of the main focuses in martial arts training is persistence. Students are taught that there will be obstacles in their training but that the end reward far outweighs any challenge. The ones who are successful in martial arts are those who refused to quit and follow through with their goals. We tell our students that a black belt is a white belt who never quit.

❝ Chris introduced me to mountain biking. Although I wasn't at his skill level, I was training hard to get there. Chris constantly talked about a mountain bike race that he was entering but never asked me to join him. It wasn't until later that I realized he was planting the seed in my subconscious. Two days before the race, Chris finally asked me to go with him. I made every excuse I could think of—my bike was in the shop, I had an appointment that day, and I had too much work—that didn't stop Chris though. The night before the race, he left a message telling me that he had already entered me in the novice race, which was "only" one nine-mile lap around a mountain. That night I couldn't sleep. All I kept thinking about was how I would feel if I didn't do the race. Then I began thinking about how I would feel if I really did compete in the race. When I showed up that Sunday morning in my T-shirt and shorts, with everyone else in racing gear, I noticed that the novice race had already started, so I decided I would race in the sport class, which was the eighteen-mile ride instead.

About half way through the race, I'm thinking to myself, 'What in the hell am I doing?' I told myself, 'I shouldn't be in the eighteen-mile race. I'm just a beginner,' so I decided to just complete the first lap and then stop. But as I finished my first lap, I saw the spectators lined up all along the finish line clapping and urging all the riders by yelling 'One more lap!' I thought about our seminars and what we teach. How could I quit when we tell others not to? So it was time to 'walk the walk.' I thought to myself just one more lap, I can do this. Only minutes later, I ran out of water, my body cramped, and I fell off of my bike. Still, I wasn't going to quit. I visualized my family standing at the finish line. I kept thinking about my wife and daughter clapping for me as I finished the race. I didn't let my body experience the pain. I just visualized the end result. And just like in the movies, a beam of sunlight broke through the trees and illuminated a Gatorade bottle. I think I even heard angels singing. Someone had dropped a full bottle during the race. I picked it up and downed it. As I was racing downhill, I hit a rock and flew through the air. A man jumped out of the bushes with a video camera and then ran away. He was recording wipeouts for his Website. Despite all of these obstacles, I kept my eye on the goal and didn't quit. I finished the race with my wife and my daughter clapping for me at the finish line. Still to this day, I remind Chris that I owe him one. **"**

—PAUL

When your desires are strong enough, you will appear to possess superhuman powers to achieve.

—NAPOLEON HILL

Will

Will is your inner strength propelling you toward success and achievement. It pushes you into action in every area of life. By asserting your will, life is filled with one accomplishment after another; which in turns helps develop more confidence in yourself. Each one of us has will; the difference is whether or not we choose to use it. Will helps you to overcome laziness, procrastination, vulnerability, lack of self-confidence, and low self-esteem. With will you are able to control compulsive or harmful impulses. It also enables you to make sound decisions, to abide by them, and to follow through with persistence until their successful accomplishment. This ability gives you the courage and strength to endure and overcome inner and outer resistance, opposition, difficulties, and hardships. Many times it is like a mental sparring match. The voices inside your head are saying to do something or not do something. When you possess a strong "Will," you can overpower the negative voice or paralyzing paradigm and follow through with your goals.

> 66 My son wanted me to attend a martial arts class with him. My first thought was 'No, I'm too old. I can't do that.' I had to recondition not only my training regimen but also my thoughts regarding age. I told myself that age is just a state of mind. It took a tremendous amount of willpower to balance my career, family, and training. My son Joseph and I pushed each other. I'll never forget the day we both received our black belt. As I held his hand, I realized how willpower and determination gave me one of the best days of my life. 99
>
> —NICK

Here's someone you might be familiar with, Christopher Gardner. Through a fierce sense of will and determination, he persisted through grave challenges to become the owner and CEO of an international corporation with offices in New York, Chicago, and San Francisco. His story was so inspiring that it became a best-selling novel and hit movie, *The Pursuit of Happyness*. His childhood was scarred by domestic violence, alcoholism, sexual abuse, and extreme poverty. He never knew his father and spent the majority of his youth in foster homes.

In 1981, he was determined to find a career that would support his son. Even though he had no college degree, he pursued a job in the financial industry. Gardner applied for training programs at brokerages, willing to live on next to nothing while he learned a new trade. Despite his circumstances, he fought to keep his son because, as he said, "I made up my mind as a young kid that when I had children they were going to know who their father is and that he isn't going anywhere."

After earning a spot in the Dean Witter Reynolds training program, he became homeless when he could not make ends meet on his meager trainee salary. From 1983 to 1987, he worked at Bear Stearns & Co. and became a top earner. In 1987, he founded the brokerage firm Gardner Rich from his home in Chicago with just $10,000. Christopher Gardner is a prime example of what can be accomplished by never giving up and utilizing one's own will, desire, and persistence.

As with self-control, developing will is a gradual process. You must formulate healthy and productive habits. Training and exercising your will gives you strength, courage, and assertiveness. As your will increases, so does your confidence, which enables you to rid your life of the bad habits, negative attitudes and paralyzing paradigms standing in your way to a better life.

WRITE A SCENARIO IN YOUR LIFE WHERE YOU USED YOUR WILL TO ACCOMPLISH A GOAL.

To be a Black Belt in the martial arts requires a burning desire and the will to overcome numerous obstacles physically, mentally and spiritually. When a student struggles on a breaking technique or some other training that they are finding difficult, we as Martial Arts Masters often become happy. Not happy that the student is struggling, but happy that when they are successful with the technique, they will have demonstrated perseverance without giving up. This is the most powerful learning experience that a martial artist and others from all walks of life could learn.

> A desire to be in charge of our own lives, a need for control, is born in each of us. It is essential to our mental health, and our success, that we take control.
>
> —ROBERT F. BENNETT

Burning Desire

Many people believe that there is no difference between desire and a burning desire. In reality, there is an enormous difference between the two. A desire is just a want or a wish, while a burning desire is a need and desire that consumes your every thought. It runs so deep that you feel it in your gut. You are driven to fulfill that need. An individual with a strong Worthy Ideal will also have a strong burning desire. Wanting and wishing aren't enough. For example, many people want to be millionaires but most of them aren't because they don't have the burning desire to do what it takes to become one.

Let's take your average "fanatical" sports fan. How successful would their lives be if they applied that same level of energy, that burning desire for their team, toward their own lives? Now don't get us wrong, all four of us are pretty avid sports fans. However, if you really think about it, sports fans are basically rooting fervently for other people to succeed, people they don't know and wouldn't benefit from if they did. Anyone who achieves their best, no matter what that is, has an unstoppable hunger lurking behind the scenes. Do you just want something or do you really want something? The question, "What do you want?" is certainly important, but the question, "How much do you want it?" is key to achieving it.

A burning desire is nothing more than a reflection of your passion for what you want. Do you really want to improve your life? Do you really want to become successful? Do you follow through on what you say you want? Are you taking the appropriate actions? This yearning creates a strong, energetic force that propels you toward your goals and fulfilling your Worthy Ideal. As a result, you make choices that are effective and even ineffective at times. It doesn't matter though, because the passion you have for achieving something continually moves you forward. You will discover what works for you and what doesn't, as long as you're paying attention.

Can you truly say that you have a burning desire to succeed in life? Take a moment and ask yourself the following questions about your desires.

1. Is it a focused desire, or am I continually distracted by some new adventure?
2. Is it a desire I am willing to make great sacrifices for?
3. What is my ultimate motivation for fulfilling this desire?

Without a burning desire, obstacles and challenges prevent you from accomplishing the success you seek. So what is burning desire, and where does it come from? A burning desire is an insatiable longing for your ideal of success. You have to want something strongly enough that you're willing to step out of your comfort zone to achieve it. Initially, this may be difficult, or you may not know how. Your burning desire needs to be so strong that the achievement of this success becomes your purpose for being. It has to be a burning desire!

We believe there are levels of desire. Everyone has a desire to achieve something. However, the people who develop this desire into a true burning desire are those who will achieve goals and be successful in life. If you had to do something for the well being of your family, would you do whatever it takes? For example, when a parent has a child with special needs, it becomes a burning desire to help him or her live the best possible life.

" My wife Kathy and I have five children. Our oldest has been diagnosed with a mild form of Aspergers. It has been a very challenging road to find the right program and school for him. The difficulties began in elementary school. In the fourth grade, he was suspended from school over thirty times. While he is extremely high functioning, speaks normally, and has the appearance of a typical child, he processes things in a unique way that is not mainstreamed or accepted by the public schools, and so he has been viewed as disrespectful and uncooperative.

Part of his disability is a misconduct disorder that makes him respond inappropriately to the teachers. For this reason, some of his teachers thought he was doing the behaviors on purpose, and he was sent to the principal on a daily basis. My wife and I spent hours defending his case because we understood that his behaviors were due to his disability and were not on purpose. My wife even went so far as to ask the teachers to find a positive in what he was doing in his classes to try to save some of our son's self-esteem. One of his teachers outright refused to do this and said that he had nothing positive to say about him.

My wife dedicated two full school years to countless meetings with the committee of special education, with student advocacy, and even hired an attorney to represent us at the CSE (Committee of Special Education) meetings. This does not include the thousands of dollars spent on psychiatric testing, therapy, and hours upon hours of preparation for the meeting my family endured. At the end of the seventh grade, it was finally determined that my son would be placed in a highly therapeutic day program to accommodate his special needs and that his behaviors were not on purpose but were in fact due to his disability. At the end of the day, my wife did whatever it took to get him in the right placement where he could experience success. It was truly her burning desire. "

—CHRIS

Those who develop their desires into a true "burning" desire are those who will ultimately be successful in life.

All of your successes must be in alignment with your desires. Your desire determines your persistence. Desire is the starting point for all of your wants in life. Keep this in mind: without a burning desire, persistence is just a word.

Persistence is a strong state of mind, built around the following causes:

1. Desire: This is the single most important element of persistence.
2. Purpose: You have to know exactly what you want and what your purpose in life is to develop persistence.
3. Positive self-image: Believing in your own abilities is crucial for persistence. When you believe in yourself, you will have the persistence to follow your dreams.
4. Organization: Your plans must be organized. The more organized you are, the easier it is to stick to your plans. By sticking to your plans with consistent action, you will build strong persistence.
5. Knowledge: Knowing what you are doing and having the skills to accomplish your tasks and goals will give you the strength and encouragement to persist in any situation in life. If you don't have the skills, either make the commitment to learn the skills or find someone with the specialized knowledge to help you.
6. Support: Support and understanding from others, most importantly your family, builds persistence through the power of faith that others have in you.
7. Habits: Good habits are the direct result of persistence. You will experience greater persistence each day through the habits you have created. Especially when they become part of your subconscious.
8. An open mind: A mind open to new ideas gives you a fresh perspective and helps to achieve higher levels of success.

{
Never let your persistence and passion turn into stubbornness and ignorance.

—ANTHONY J. D'ANGELO
}

The Skill of Persistence

Developing the skill of persistence makes up for our deficiencies in all the other areas. It will allow us to be a winner in life no matter what obstacles are placed in front of us. Persistence levels the playing field. To have the ability to move forward and meet the challenge when everything around you is collapsing is empowering. We all aspire to be professional. For example, take the average salesperson who spends three hours cold calling for new clients. Even though they don't feel like making those telephone calls, they continue to dial. Many of us know what we need to do, yet we choose not to do it. Almost all people are looking for a short cut, the quick buck. Very few of us want to get our hands dirty. We spend our time looking for the one step that will change our life, rather than using the path of persistence to win. Some people in society today want something for nothing—consider those late night commercials promising overnight riches or instant weight loss with no effort. There is no magic pill to solve all of our problems.

Will $\longrightarrow$ Burning Desire $\longrightarrow$ Persistence $\longrightarrow$ Success

Now, we want to make a little point about success. Success is however you define it. There is no right or wrong. We can tell you that success will be a continuous journey throughout life. You will never get to a certain point in your life and say, "Now I am successful." We have had clients who experienced success in certain areas of life, like business or money, but were also overweight and had poor health and vitality. We've also coached clients who were highly spiritual but couldn't pay their bills. To us, both do not demonstrate success. Success should be experienced in all areas of life and ultimately should create happiness within your life's journey.

You have to work before you receive the reward.

66 In 1999, my martial arts school was growing, and it needed to relocate. I didn't want to pay rent, but I couldn't find any commercial real estate within my budget. About a mile from my studio was a vacant building with a For Sale sign. It needed a lot of work. I met with the real estate broker. He mentioned that the price was $350,000. I went

to the tax office to find the owners and negotiate a deal. The couple listed on the deed as the owners lived in Florida. When I called to ask about the building, I was told it wasn't for sale. I mentioned the For Sale sign on the building and that I was interested in buying. It turned out that the tenants leasing the building were trying to sell it without the owner's knowledge. The owner explained that her husband had owned the property but left it to her when he passed away. She was in litigation with her tenants, was paying taxes on the building, and was not getting any rental income from it. She explained that she couldn't sell me the property until the litigation was over and asked how much the tenants were trying to sell the building for. 'Three hundred and fifty-thousand dollars,' I replied. 'Well, when this is done,' she told me, 'I will sell it to you for two hundred and fifty thousand dollars. But you have to speak with my attorney.' After a few more phone calls, she finally gave me her attorney's name and number. I called, and the attorney ignored me.

So, I decided to call both the attorney and the owner every week. I did this for one year. One day, the owner was so frustrated with paying her taxes, paying attorney fees, and not receiving any rental income that she sold me the building for $100,000. **"**

—PAUL

Persistence starts with one step at a time. You need to have a vision of what you want. If you want to change your financial situation, the first step is to assess your finances. There is a great saying, "What gets measured gets managed. You cannot change your finances if you don't even know where your finances are. You can't expect to wake up one morning deciding to be rich and go to bed as a millionaire. Such a thought process certainly sets you up for failure. Remember, there is no magic pill. You have to set goals and stick with them. Your desire for wealth will come true if you practice persistence on a daily basis. Start by selecting one action item you need to do today in order to obtain your financial goal, and then make sure you complete it before the end of the day. Don't ever end your day before you get it done.

The best way to learn persistence is to start. This sounds easy enough, but it is the biggest barrier for most people. The anticipation is the worst part. As with most activities in life, the first time is never as bad as our minds make it out to be. Once you begin, you pick up both momentum and the positive self-talk of accomplishment. Persistence is the skill that we need to master. It is the one skill that helps us achieve success in both our personal and professional life. Describe a time in your life where you used persistance to get what you wanted.

> To make our way, we must have firm resolve, persistence, tenacity. We must gear ourselves to work hard all the way. We can never let up.
>
> —RALPH BUNCHE

Pursue

Recall that Thomas Edison failed ten thousand times before he invented the light bulb. How could someone have patience to fail that many times when people told him it was impossible? Today, we hear so many examples of people who quit after their first failure. Jerry Jones, the owner of the Dallas Cowboys, became a billionaire by drilling in a location where someone else had already given up. He drilled one time and struck oil. What did Thomas Edison have that these people don't? He knew how to PURSUE his burning desire. To PURSUE you must:

Persist Until Reaching Strong Undeniable Effects

Successful people believe in themselves and their pursuits. All successful people fail at one time or another in their life, so what is the difference between you and them? They don't have the word failure in their dictionary and they turn failures into learning experiences. From this day forward, remove failure from your vocabulary because you only fail when you quit. Successful people have the ability to keep their eyes and focus on the prize, and to never allow the obstacles and challenges to block their vision.

So how do you PURSUE what you want in life? How can you develop an unshakable persistence that keeps you moving forward no matter how many times you fail? Find and work toward your purpose in life, your Worthy Ideal. Once you discover your true purpose in life, you become unstoppable. Following your Worthy Ideal or Life's Purpose will give you a sense of your own existence, and by doing what you love, you will make a difference and add value to the world around you.

Your purpose fuels your inspiration no matter how long the journey is or how many times you fail.

CHAPTER SUMMARY

- Persistence empowers you to overcome obstacles and challenges.
- Will pushes you to strive for the best you can be.
- A burning desire is more than just a want in life.
- Successful people persist while others walk away.
- Without a burning desire, persistence is just a word.

CHAPTER FIVE

Self-Image

> Science and psychology have isolated the one prime cause for success or failure in life. It is the hidden self-image you have of yourself.
>
> **—BOB PROCTOR**

Self-image is defined as how you perceive yourself. It can inhibit or empower you. Without a good self-image, it's easy to capitulate to others who try to break you down with harsh criticism. Because of their remarks, you berate yourself and take things personally, rather than viewing it as constructive criticism about you or your behavior. A positive self-image instills confidence in who you are and what you can achieve.

Conversely, you lack a positive self-image, you fall prey to others' judgments of you. Constantly worrying what everyone thinks translates into negative thoughts, like not asking for and therefore not getting what you want in life. So let's delve into your mind, your own perception of who you are, and see what your self-image looks like.

Below is a short questionnaire about your self-image. Read through each statement and mark either true or false. Remember, be honest with yourself. This book is for your personal development, so answer the questions based on how you feel, not on how you think you should feel. These exercises will help you to tap into your infinite power, but only if you answer them with the utmost honesty.

STATEMENT	TRUE	FALSE
I admit my mistakes.		
I stand behind my values even if others disagree with me.		
I am comfortable spending time alone.		
I affirm myself and others.		
I easily accept compliments from others.		
I can reach out to those around me without fear.		
I accept my faults.		
I am happy for other's successes.		

I am calm and possess an
inner peace.

I love who I am.

I am open with my feelings for
other people.

I don't compare myself with others.

I believe I have something to offer
to others.

I don't care what other people think
of me.

I accept all people without
judgment.

I don't change my personality to suit
others.

I am not afraid to admit my faults as
well as my strengths.

If you answered true to most of the questions, then you have a good self-image. If not, don't worry; it can easily be fixed. As a matter of fact, a person's self-image generally is always evolving as we go through different stages of our lives.

Keeping up with the Joneses

Do you compare your weaknesses to other people's strengths? Sometimes you
might develop a low self-image by constantly judging yourself against others.
You look at other people's successes and accomplishments and say, "I can't
do that." You're in competition with your neighbors, relatives, friends, and
coworkers. Or perhaps you look at others with envy and wonder why you aren't
as successful as they are. You ask yourself, "What do they have that I don't?"
There is so much pressure in society today to keep up with the Joneses. You
want desperately to attain some aspect of their life: their car, their house, or
their clothes. This is so evident with the pressures that our children are under.
For example, approximately 31 percent of teenage girls in the United States
have an eating disorder. They look at models and celebrities and instantly feel
bad, not taking into account that the majority of the pictures or images they see
have somehow been altered through digital photography or lighting.

Keeping up with the Joneses is seductive. It's like gambling—sometimes
you win, but more often than not you lose. In the end, you feel inadequate or
inferior to the people you are comparing yourself to. It's okay to admire people;
unfortunately, most people make the mistake of envying them. Take a moment
and look at yourself introspectively and answer the following questions.

I'm not _____ enough compared to _____

I'm not _____ enough compared to _____

I'm not _____ enough compared to _____

I'm not _____ enough compared to _____

What did you discover about yourself? Is keeping up with the Joneses robbing you of your self-image? We want to share with you something we learned a long time ago—something so basic, so obvious, yet overlooked by most people. There will always be someone with more money, a bigger house, a nicer car, or a better job than us. There will always be someone who is thinner, more muscular, or better looking. The list is endless. Everything is relative. No matter who you are, someone inevitably will have more than you. But that's okay. That's the way life is. Fortunately the converse is true as well. That is, no matter what you think you don't have, there will always be someone who has less. There will always be someone who is envious of you as well. So, the sooner you stop comparing yourself to others, the sooner you will be on your way to a better self-image.

As you improve your self-image, everything around you begins to change. Emotionally you feel better, and confidence soon follows, allowing you to pursue your goals and dreams in life. You come to believe that you deserve everything you desire in life. Your attitude conveys a strong sense of self-assurance, and as other people see you in this new light, they can't help but agree as well.

So, how is your mind programmed to see things? Let's do a quick test.

What do you see in the picture below? Do you see an old lady or a young one?

" I recently conducted a ten-week coaching program on self-image for professional women. In the first session, I showed her the above photo. She was only able to see an old, ugly woman. Ironically, from her original perspective, everything in her life was in shambles. She wasn't happy with how much money she was making or with her physical appearance. Her relationships with family and friends weren't where she wanted them to be, and ultimately, she always attracted the wrong guy into her life. She caught herself complaining about everything. During the two months that she and I worked together, we reconditioned her mind regarding how she viewed life and began applying our teaching concepts. It wasn't until the eighth visit that I asked her to go back to review an exercise I had her do in her journal. Next to that exercise was that picture of the lady. She began to cry, because that was the first time she really saw the beautiful young lady. Her mind had shifted. She'd started seeing the good in herself. "

—PAUL

DESCRIBE IN DETAIL WHAT TYPE OF QUALITIES YOU WANT IN A PERSON. (FAMILY-ORIENTED, RESPECTFUL, HONEST)

1.

2.

3.

4.

5.

6.

7.

8.

9.

10.

WHAT KIND OF SELF-IMAGE DO YOU NEED TO ATTRACT THIS TYPE OF PERSON INTO YOUR LIFE?

Did the qualities above match your self-image? If those attributes don't match your current opinion of yourself, then it will be difficult to find that someone you're looking for. Like attracts like, so you can't attract your ideal mate until you first love yourself.

We have worked with many people who were able to turn their lives around and become successful by starting with a simple change in how they perceive themselves. At first, they were uncertain who they really were and what they wanted to accomplish. By focusing on their good qualities and visualizing themselves as the person they always wanted to be, their confidence level slowly increased. Others began to recognize their efforts and achievements. One of the most rewarding experiences from teaching seminars and workshops is knowing we can help improve someone's life for the better.

The woman in the story above learned how to see the good in herself, but it wasn't until she valued and loved herself that she was able to marry a man with all the qualities she was looking for. In our seminars, we teach the philosophy that what you think about is what you become; if you believe in yourself and have a confident self-image, then there are no limits to what you can achieve. You need to start out with that belief, which helps to create the experiences to support it. Of course, external circumstances and certain situations can help you accomplish certain goals, but if you lack a good self-image, all the favorable circumstances in the world won't give you that feeling of empowerment you need for continued success.

Once you develop a positive self-image, you gain an "I can do anything" feeling and are ready to take on new responsibilities, which lead to personal growth. If you believe that you can achieve a particular goal, then once you know you can do it, you can. It all comes back to belief. You must believe and know that you have the power to create the life you want, and then that belief will empower you to follow through.

The key to improving your self-image is to overcome fears, anxieties, self-doubts, and limiting beliefs like "I can't do it" or "I'm not good enough." You have to focus on what you can do, on knowing you can do it, and on seeing yourself doing it. Whenever we think about what we do well, it's a form of self-affirmation that builds our self-image.

The following Conditioning Exercise is a good way to evaluate your self-image. Take some time and search introspectively before writing and, as with the previous Success Conditioning Exercises, make certain your answers are honest. Perhaps have your significant other do this as well. If you have teenage children, then they should also join in.

	What is your current self image regarding...	How do you want to improve yourself image regarding...
Your physical appearance?		
Your family		
Your friends		
Your career		

Did you learn something about your self-image? How about your significant other or your kids? Did it match what you want to be? If not, don't worry because whatever your results, you're already one step ahead of most people simply by doing this exercise in the first place. Most people never look introspectively to improve. If you don't have the characteristics that you want now, you can develop them. Remember, it is all about belief. If you believe, then you can have those characteristics; you'll develop them, and your self-image will improve. If that belief turns into knowing, then you will have jumped to the head of the class.

Your self-image is what you see when you look in the mirror. You either like yourself or you don't. If you don't like who you see in the mirror, it's probably difficult to trust yourself, or anyone else for that matter. Here's another exercise that will prove useful. Use the space below to list your talents and abilities. Now don't be bashful. Believe us when we say you do have talents and abilities.

LIST TEN TALENTS AND ABILITIES.

1.

2.

3.

4.

5.

6.

7.

8.

9.

10.

How did you do with this exercise? Very often people with a poor self-image have difficulty identifying their talents and abilities. They don't believe they have anything to offer the world. Was it hard for you to complete your list? If so, again, don't worry. There are no failing grades here. We're here to lend you a guiding hand.

Let's show you how to replace your old beliefs with new positive ones about yourself. The first step is to affirm what you want to get and then truly believe it. In the latter portion of this book, we define affirmations as our "Mind Muscle Exercises." Remember that even if you don't have that quality now, by truly believing, you will become the person you want to be. The qualities must align with the person you want to become in your lifetime.

Here's an example: Each morning I affirm the following in my life:

I am loving

I am thankful

I am grateful

I am appreciative

I am passionate

I am focused

I am determined

I am persistent

I am confident

I am financially free and abundant

I am wealthy

I am fun

I am happy

I am internally vital

I am physically flexible

—PAUL

IN THE SPACE BELOW, WRITE YOUR OWN AFFIRMATIONS
ABOUT WHO YOU ARE OR WHAT YOU WANT TO BE. MAKE CER-
TAIN TO WRITE THEM IN PRESENT TENSE. AFTER ALL, THINKING
IS ONE OF THE MAIN PURPOSES OF THIS BOOK, AND WE ALL
MUST BE ABLE TO DO IT TO ATTAIN INFINITE POWER.
WHAT ARE YOUR AFFIRMATIONS? BE SURE TO BEGIN YOUR
AFFIRMATION WITH I AM...

I AM...

When you say these "I AM" statements, communicate with your whole body. Speaking these words alone is only 7 percent effective. Altering your tonality increases your words' effectiveness 38 percent, while adding body language increases it by 55 percent. A more enthusiastic and focused body language makes your words much more powerful. Think about how you tell someone "I love you." Do you mumble the words and look away? Or do you take them into your arms, smile, and tell them? There must be a gesture with each "I AM" statement; otherwise it doesn't have the same effect. A slow, drawn out tone says it, but it's not believable. When you condition a hand gesture for each "I AM" statement, then you anchor it in your mind.

Remember, any time you attach the words "I AM" to a statement, you become it. Select your most important affirmation and focus on it for about a minute. Now, repeat your "I AM" over and over to yourself for two to three minutes. As you do this, see the statement you have written in your mind's eye. Don't just hear or see the words. Translate your message into a visual image. Practice this technique once a day for the next twenty-one days, and soon you'll notice feeling better about yourself and that things you want are coming into your life. Don't just take our word for it; take it from one of the most famous personalities of the twentieth century: Muhammad Ali.

Muhammad Ali was very animated and passionate with his words. The most powerful statement that illustrates our point is his famous affirmation, "I am the greatest!" He told everyone who was willing to listen that he was the greatest. He said it with such conviction that soon even his opponents believed him. It was so powerful that he intimidated many of his opponents before they ever entered the ring.

Affirmations are a powerful tool because they lead to a subtle attitude change that transforms your belief and affects how you feel about yourself. As they build your self-image, adding visualization to them further increases the magnitude of your beliefs. This process works because you not only make yourself more aware of who you are, but also feel what it is like to be successful, healthy, wealthy, or whatever you want in life by visualizing it. You're using mental imagery to convince yourself that you are experiencing what you want in the present, and your feelings and actions respond to complement and reinforce that mental image.

One of the greatest benefits of being a martial arts instructor is to see our students both young and old develop a martial arts mindset. This is when they take on the identity of a martial artist and all of their thoughts funnel through the five tenets of taekwondo; Perseverance, Self Control, Indomitable Spirit, Respect, and Integrity. One who has the self-image of a martial artist has the ability to filter their challenges through the five tenets and find the best solution.

66 Early in my career, I envisioned myself as the president of the executive committee of a major insurance company. I held that vision in my mind throughout my career and in 2001, I was voted by my peers as the president of the executive committee. As I gave my acceptance speech in front of two thousand people, I realized the power of I AM statements. 99

—NICK

By focusing on and visualizing what you want, you will experience life-altering transformations. The following Conditioning for Success Exercise should be repeated once a day for twenty-one days to reinforce and strengthen your self-image. Later, you can turn these feelings into reality by initiating new actions to implement your vision.

- Affirming and visualizing your abilities and talents, and seeing yourself as an abundant, successful person helps you to take full control of your life.
- Decide what you want most out of life.
- Close your eyes and visualize yourself realizing this goal.
- Make your image of this achievement as vivid as possible, and see your success happening.
- As you visualize your success, experience the satisfaction and feeling of power this brings.

- Feel elated, excited, strong, powerful, fully self-confident, and in charge. Visualize others meeting you or calling to congratulate you. You feel warm and glowing as you receive their praise. They tell you how successful you are.
- Feel wonderful, and have the confidence to be able to do anything you want.

You need to decide the self-image most suited for you both personally and professionally. Previously, we asked if the self-image you want matches your current one. If it doesn't, then you have to identify the areas you want to develop further to get closer to your Worthy Ideal. Determine what you want to become. Ask yourself: "How would I like to improve?" However you want to, the Conditioning for Success Exercises we presented can help you imagine which qualities to eliminate and which to develop. Once you decide who you want to be, rehearse the role over and over again in your mind until you reinforce the reality of this new image. Soon, you'll see the new you.

66 We have several young adults who work for us. We designed a leadership program to help them take on leadership roles. Most kids are trying to find themselves. They'll do anything for acceptance. Their image among their peers is very important. They don't care if it's positive or negative; they just want to fit in. We want them to have a healthy self-image. Our program has made a difference in the lives of several of our young employees. 99

—CHRIS AND PAUL

Now take the new image you have created and put it into practice in real-life situations. The process of creating a new self-image is much like the process of targeting goals (discussed in Chapter 11). Initially, you think about who you want to become, and then decide which qualities are most important to you so that you can work on achieving them first.

CHAPTER SUMMARY

- A positive self-image is easily developed once we stop comparing ourselves to others.
- As self-image improves, so does confidence.
- Use "I am" statements to affirm your positive self-image.
- Visualize the image you want and firmly plant it in your subconscious mind.
- A firm, positive self-image enables you to take on more responsibilities.

CHAPTER SIX

Focus

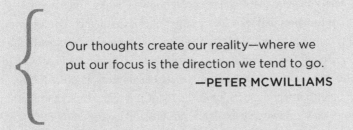

Our thoughts create our reality—where we put our focus is the direction we tend to go.
—**PETER MCWILLIAMS**

This step in our T.R.A.N.S.F.O.R.M.A.T.I.O.N. Doctrine is one of the most difficult disciplines to learn and master. The concept and art of focusing is nothing new. In the Korean martial art of Taekwondo, a series of choreographed moves against an imaginary opponent is used to teach trainees to defend themselves. This is known as *poomse*, which is a Korean term for patterns or forms. We practice *poomse* daily during our training to help our students develop the art of focus. The practice of *poomse* originates with ancient warriors who, after witnessing battle techniques that worked, returned home and intently practiced the methods until they became automatic. In their world, success meant staying alive, so they had to focus and practice these moves to survive.

In this chapter, we're going to focus on focus. Ironically, while writing this chapter, we had challenges and couldn't focus on focusing. We found this chapter the most difficult to complete. Between Nick constantly messaging on his cell phone and Chris' spontaneous laughter, it's a wonder we finished at all. So try your best to stay with us here. Make sure to turn off your cell phone and avoid your own spontaneous fits of laughter.

In all seriousness, we truly believe that the scientific aspect of the discipline of focus is vital to your success. You have to passionately concentrate and focus your time, talents, creativity, and energy in order to achieve the goals you set for yourself. (More about goals in Chapter 11.)

With a determined focus, the mind releases untapped energy and magnifies all of your capabilities. When you priortize positive energy and relentlessly focus on your goals, you create your own destiny. But staying focused is a continuous challenge, as we experienced first hand. This chapter was quite a learning experience for us. Paul used a pre-meditation technique to help us regain our focus. (Meditation is detailed in Chapter 9.) First we had to get rid of our frustration and maintain a state of calmness. Paul told us to concentrate our attention on one spot in the room and to focus on our breathing. With each breath, we slowly released our tensions and excess energy to the point where our minds were clear and our emotions calm.

Martial arts are perhaps one of the best disciplines for developing focus. We teach people of all ages how to focus with amazing success. When we give seminars to schools and corporations, we use the analogy of being like a laser to harness and focus energy on the task at hand. Now, we'd like to share these principles with you.

Principle 1: Focus on progress, not perfection.
1. Compete with yourself.
2. If you are always focused on where you want to go, then you will experience success.
3. Appreciate the journey while you focus on your accomplishments, and you will have the confidence to move toward your destination.

Principle 2: Focus on the positive.
1. You have to make the choice.
2. Choose to find the positive in any situation because there always is one. Be a good finder.

Principle 3: Focus time.
1. Focus on what you want.
2. Set aside a time every week as your "focus day" when you focus on your unique abilities.
3. Be present and eliminate all distractions.
4. Spend the majority of this designated day working on focused "Action Steps" that will assist you in attaining your goals or objectives.

The result of following these three principles is more productivity in less time. This will leave you more free time to do the leisure activities you enjoy, like exercising or spending time with family and friends.

The art of breaking a stack of boards or a cinderblock with your hand or foot is possible through determined focus and concentration. Ever wonder how kids half your weight and strength can break a stack of boards or blocks? It's all about mastering the art and discipline of focusing your mind like a laser on one specific objective. Anybody who wants to live in health and vitality must win the constant battle of temptation to sleep in rather than to work out. Staying focused on the way you want to live your life will help you win this battle. Distractions, disappointments, and interruptions interfere with our lives on a daily basis. If you find your enthusiasm diminishing or disappearing during this battle of your mind, then you'll have to implement the three principles below, which will help you stay focused from start to finish.

Your energy flows where your attention goes.

Three essential ingredients are needed to stay focused.
1. Burning desire
2. Endurance
3. Patience

The Science of Focus

Okay we're going to get technical here, so let's put our focus to the test. Block out all distractions. Pretend you're in a movie theater and turn your cell phone off. Let's see how far you get. Metaphysical teachings state that by intensely focusing your expectation on a desired result, you physically realign the signal that the energies created by your emotions and imagination send—which then permeate everything within the universe. This signal then attracts energy that matches your projection of thought, resulting in the manifestation of the conditions you imagine. Have you ever mentioned someone's name only to see them hours later? Or have you ever had a bad day only to have it continue to worsen? What about a good day that only gets better? Scientific evidence has proven how expectancy and assumptions change our biochemistry. Fear and anxiety, for example, depress the immune system while optimistic attitudes seem to improve immune function. In other words, what you focus your thoughts on can actually alter some of your brainwaves, giving you a better ability to turn your thoughts into reality.

Science has also proven the powerful effects of the placebo response. This undeniable healing response is activated when individuals believe they have been given a powerful drug but are actually taking something with no scientifically acknowledged active ingredient. From the mind-body perspective, belief is the active ingredient in the placebo response—or any treatment. Strong belief in a cure can be a catalyst for shifting our attention—our unconscious visualizations—from a focus on sickness to one that allows healing.

❝ When I was 13, I started having painful stomachaches. I would wake up at night bent over in severe agony and these pains continued to occur at the same time each night. They were so intense that I would wake up in a sweat. The only way I could ease the pain was to sit up in bed bent over. After a while I would eventually fall asleep in this position. In the morning the pain would mysteriously be gone, only to return again that night. My parents took me to the emergency room several times, where I was poked and prodded everywhere with no result. Finally after a few weeks, my doctor admitted me to the hospital to run more tests. Still, they couldn't find what was wrong and the stomach pains persisted. One morning, my doctor came in along with my parents and told me they'd finally found out what was wrong. He gave me some medical explanation I didn't understand. What got my attention was when he told me he was giving me pills to take the pain away, and they would make me feel better in a matter of hours. I readily took the pills and have never had the pains since. I slept through the night and was released from the hospital the very next day. I remember thinking that my doctor was a medical genius. It wasn't until many months later that my father told me the pills were sugar tablets, a placebo. I was blown away. As a side note, for many years thereafter and occasionally to this day, I would still wake up in the middle of the night only to fall back asleep sitting up. My wife says, 'Now I know what it's like to see someone sleepwalking. You think they're awake and talk to them, only to realize they're in a deep sleep and can't hear a word you're saying.' **"**

—RICK

Repetition is often a by-product of strong belief, since you tend to return mentally to thinking about and picturing anticipated results. But the shift in belief that changes your feelings is the catalyst in using visualization for change. Why do you have to keep repeating this mantra if you really believe you'll get well? Couldn't you just go about the business of healing without belaboring the matter? If you can believe with absolute conviction in a completely new way of being, one energetically charged vision of this desired self can be enough to set you on the path of improvement.

Most people think the mind is an organ. We, on the contrary, believe the mind is an activity.

Brain is a noun and Mind is a verb.

Most people believe that we are physical beings having a spiritual experience. We, however, believe that we are spiritual beings having a physical experience and that our bodies are just the manifestation of the activity of our minds. All your active beliefs propel your feelings. To us, our health is one of the main focuses we should have. For example, take a patient's belief that something outside of them—a drug—could cure them. This promotes feelings of hope, optimism, and confidence. Please don't misunderstand us; prescription drugs are necessary in many circumstances, and we certainly aren't advising in any way to discontinue the use of any medications. We do want, however, to explore the connection between healing and a positive attitude. To achieve healing, you must be mentally prepared to make the necessary changes to receive it.

You must maintain a positive attitude toward healing to achieve it. Attitude is everything; change it and apply those changes necessary for healing in your life. Make your attitude, your mental position, a positive one to get the results. A positive attitude is a healing attitude! The following diagram is a good example of the connection between attitude and health.

Negative attitude ➝ Toxins ➝ Stress ➝ Disease

Positive attitude ➝ Appreciation ➝ Energy ➝ Body at ease

There is no question that the things we think have a tremendous effect upon our bodies. If we can change our thinking, the body frequently heals itself.

—C. EVERETT KOOP, M.D.

The Mind-Body Connection

Your personal mind-body connection and the interactions among your thoughts, body, and social environment are an integral part of beginning to achieve focus in your life. Scientists, philosophers, and religious thinkers have developed theories and adhered to a wide variety of beliefs on the subject. Is a person's body simply a physical entity, separate from the mind and controlled by biochemical reactions and environmental stimuli? Or can one's thoughts and feelings wield a power over one's body? Can the body's own physical qualities affect thoughts and emotions?

As stated at the beginning of this chapter, we practice poomse. This technique develops the mind-body connection as students learn to focus on each movement of their hands, feet, arms, and legs. The mind and body work as one to achieve the desired results. When a person begins training, they feel awkward and uncomfortable. Why is this? Because they've not yet developed this mind-body connection. Learning to ski or snowboard is a great example of this. A novice skier or snowboarder lacks this connection. Once they develop this skill, the sport becomes effortless, and they feel as if they're floating.

The term mind-body connection covers two separate but related ideas. On the one hand, it refers to the belief that thoughts and emotions have an influence on whether people maintain overall physical health and also on whether and/or how quickly and completely they recover from illness. On the other side of the mind-body connection is the reverse effect: the influence that biochemical events in the body, particularly those taking place in the brain, exert over human emotions, mental state, and behavior.

Although many people use the terms mind and brain almost interchangeably, they refer to two related but different aspects of the same thing. The brain is the physical organ that houses the mind, while the mind is where thoughts, emotions, and perceptions occur. The brain is a part of the central nervous system and is divided into parts. Like all other organs in the body, its functions and activities are the end result of many complex biochemical and electrical interactions. Much has been discovered about how these biochemical processes work, but this area of science still contains many mysteries. Certain types of physical conditions in the brain correspond to certain types of mental states.

The term "mind" is often understood to refer to the thoughts, emotions, and perceptions that you actually experience. Suppose, for example, you are looking at a photograph of a friend. While this is happening, you are unaware of the millions of biochemical reactions taking place that enable you to recognize the picture and to respond to it. However the only item you actually are aware of is the picture of your friend. Though the workings of the mind are very complex, they are so natural to us that we are unaware of them, and until we achieve that awareness, we cannot alter how our minds work.

Board breaking is an important part of training that requires precise placement of your hand or foot executed with power to successfully break a board or cement. If the student loses focus, they are in danger of hurting themselves and the person holding the board. Many times we have seen young children accomplish a particular break where an adult failed. It has nothing to do with size and strength and has everything to do with focus and technique. Through martial arts training, students are taught to focus all their concentrated energy to accomplish the task at hand. When applied outside the martial arts, adults have more focus at work and home whereas children are more focused at school.

> You cannot control what happens to you, but you can control your attitude toward what happens to you, and in that, you will be mastering change rather than allowing it to master you.
>
> —BRIAN TRACY

Self-Control

Self-control is a foundation of focus. It can be both physical and mental. Physical and mental self-control makes up a total mind-body connection. It will come about with lots of repetition and practice, but it improves as time goes on. Hard work and dedication push you toward your focus.

For the average person, mental self-control is a skill that needs to be harnessed and developed. There is so much confrontation in our society and most of it comes from a lack of mental control. So many people feel the need to hear themselves speak when they should actually be listening. We must gain the ability to control our reactions, so we can see things from another person's point of view. People react without thinking and talk to hear themselves talk. A disagreement is nothing more than one person trying to convince the other that his or her point of view is correct.

If someone says something negative to you, you have to decide how to react. If you react in haste, then the situation can escalate, and there can be a strong confrontation. If you are able to control your reaction and analyze why the person is acting this way, then you will probably be able to coast through the situation and find common ground. The amount of self-control necessary in these types of scenarios can be enormous. We have to remember that when an argument or tempers flare, no one wins. We have to act as a stream flowing through a rocky bed. If there is a rock or a tree blocking the flow, the water will find a way around the obstacle. It is not going to entertain or stress over the obstacle. It is just going to flow around it as if it wasn't there. Don't put up mental resistance and entertain another person's negativity or anger. Let it roll off and float away.

Self-control at work is another method to give you an edge in your chosen career. People will always try to pull ahead of you and be the best they can be. Most people are looking out for their own best interests and have no qualms about stepping on someone else's toes to do so. We've all come across people who are always happy and positive and people who are constantly negative and complaining. When you find yourself confronted with a negative person, think about what they are saying. Is it worth wasting your time and energy on them? We like to call these people time bandits. They steal your time. Explain to them that you will work better as a team than if you always disagree. This kind of reaction states to them that you are willing to work together while still explaining how you could contribute to the solution of the challenge. Don't let anyone steal your time. Remember, everything is energy and negative people suck the energy right out of us, so first try to help them to see the good in life and others, but if you can't, then avoid them. Be "good" finders, be the leader. But if they don't change, then they're going to drag you down with them. Avoid or spend less time with them.

> " I developed a life skills program for underprivileged teenagers in Westchester County, NY, called Power Time. Most of the teenagers who participate in the program come from broken homes, and some have had serious addictions and challenges in life. You can see when interacting with many of these teens that they have already lost hope. They would walk into our meeting room with their heads down, angry at the world. I would gather them into a circle and would try to start each session with a positive focus. It was a huge struggle for everyone, but I refused to give up. Slowly but surely, some of the kids would start smiling and talking about what went well that day. Now, almost all of them walk into our Power Time sessions with smiles and hugs, and can't wait to talk about the positive things that happened to them during the week. This has been one of the most rewarding experiences in my life. "
>
> —RICK

We must also remember that different people handle stress or pressure in different ways. For example, while you're working toward a relaxed life and a life of calmness and tranquility, others may have a straw in their wallet or purse so they can suck the life right out of you. We like to call these people energy leeches. With them, we have to gain control and not let their negativity and stress affect us and how we feel. We control how we feel; therefore we should control our actions and reactions. When you meet an energy leech, smile and explain that you completely respect their opinion and want to look at the situation from both sides to find a solution. Once again, as with the time bandits, follow the same steps mentioned earlier. Explain to them, "We'll work better as a team than if we always disagree." We realize this is sometimes easier to say than do. However, we are looking to live our life with black belt character, to always find a peaceful yet productive resolution. Having enough self-control means maintaining a positive state of mind. As mentioned in the previous chapter, like attracts like, so people who are more focused and positive attract the same.

Self-control is a key ingredient for healthy and lasting relationships. When you are married and have children, the natural tendency is to spend a lot of time with your spouse and family. Developing the art of self-control will help to get through the inevitable disputes and disagreements. Sometimes we will take things for granted and not listen to the individuals closest to us. For a healthy relationship with your life partner, you must always be willing to listen to what they have to say. For example, think about the importance of listening thoroughly before reacting. Because you are so comfortable with your spouse or significant other, you may tend to react more irrationally than with a coworker. Be sure to listen to what they say and most importantly respect it. Even if you do not agree, try your best to see their perspective. Most troubled relationships have inability to communicate at their center. Have the black belt self-control to listen before you speak. It is not always easy. As with everything, it takes hard work and commitment.

Self-control should be applied in every aspect of your life. Remember to always listen and search a little deeper about why something is happening before there is a reaction. If you do this, then you will be a happier and calmer person, and others will look toward you as someone who is level headed and well balanced.

> Focus on your potential instead of your limitations.
>
> —ALAN LOY MCGINNIS

Focus Your Energy

The ability to focus harnesses your energy on one specific area or topic like a laser beam. Think of the sun's energy. If we lay out in the sun on a hot, summer day, then we can get a golden tan. But, if we use a magnifying glass on the sun's light, we can burn a hole in our arm. When we harness our attention and focus on a certain person, area of life, topic, or life purpose, then we become that laser. A key factor pertaining to energy that we all must understand is that we only have a certain amount of mental energy at our disposal at any one time. If we focus our mental energy on others or what we don't want in life, then we won't have enough left to use for our own benefit. During our seminars, many of our clients tell us what they don't want. For example, "I don't want to be broke," or "I don't want to be sick," or "I don't want to fail in business." Our task is to get them to focus their energy or attention on what they do want in life. We inspire them to say, "I am financially free and abundant," or "I am healthy and vital," or "I am a successful business owner."

Think of all the areas of your life. If you had a set "focus time" for each one, how much do you think you could improve? How much time is wasted during your day by not being focused? Learn to block out scheduled times during your day or week for your most important areas. Let's review some important aspects.

Areas of Life
1. Health & Vitality
2. Family (meaning your immediate family/close relatives)
3. Relationships (your relationship with your spouse, partner or significant other
4. Physical Appearance
5. Money
6. Work
7. Spirituality
8. Social
9. Organizational Discipline
10. Charity
11. Learning & Growth
12. Mind Development
13. Fun Activities
14. Technology

Which is more important to you, health or money? Is spirituality more important than relationships? Now arrange the areas of your life in an order of importance with one being the most important and fourteen being the least. Remember there is no wrong answer. It's your life!

LIST THE AREAS OF YOUR LIFE IN ORDER OF IMPORTANCE.

1.

2.

3.

4.

5.

6.

7.

8.

9.

10.

11.

12.

13.

14.

Now arrange the Areas of Life below into 2 categories. In the second column list how you are CURRENTLY devoting most of your time in order of importance from highest priority to lowest priority.

For example, are you spending all your time working and making money? Or, is it with your family and relationships?

Then in the third column do the same process this time listing how you would LIKE your Areas of Life to be in order of importance. In each column simply designate a number 1-14.

Remember, there is no wrong answer. Everybody is different. It's your life.

Once you have your list of importance, we recommend you take your top four which we call your CORE FOUR and choose three activities you can do every day, week, month, or year to improve that area. Create a menu of daily action steps that will help you increase the results in that area of life. This way, if you can't do one particular action step that day, you can easily choose another and still feel fulfilled.

Remember the Action Steps you choose must be specific. For example, let's say one of your CORE FOUR Areas of Life is Health & Vitality. An Action Step shouldn't be simply to work out. After all, if you lift weights for 5 minutes you don't say, "I'm in shape; I don't have to work out anymore," do you? Of course not. You need to be more detailed; how long do you want to work out, what days, what time, etc.

For your other areas of life, only choose one activity you can do each day or week to improve that area. If you put your attention and focus toward that area, you will see it dramatically improve, and you will create balance and harmony within your life. Below are Paul's examples:

AREA OF LIFE	How you have been devoting your life	How would you like to devote your life
Health & Vitality		
Family		
Relationships		
Physical Appearance		
Money		
Work		
Spirituality		
Social		
Organizational Discipline		

Charity

Learning &
Growth

Mind
Development

Fun Activities

Technology

AREA	FOCUS ACTIVITY
Health and Vitality	a. Drink half my body weight in distilled water b. Eat organic vegetables c. Drink wild green tea
Relationship	a. Tell my wife "I love you" when I wake up b. Slow dance before work c. date night at Winery
Family	a. Call mom after work b. Eat Sunday dinner with family c. Read 30 minutes with kids
Physical Appearance	a. 60 minutes Martial art training b. Cross Fit class c. Mountain Bike 10 miles
Money	a. Set up automatic withdrawal for investment b. collect rent from tenants c. Adjust net worth monthly
Spirituality	Meditate 60 minutes
Mind Development	Say my Mind Muscle Exercises in the morning

Work	30 minute staff meetings before we begin our workday
Fun Activities	Snowboarding weekend in VT
Learning and Growth	Read 30 minutes before bed
Organizational Discipline	Clean and organize desk before leaving the office
Charity	Volunteer and donate Bully Proof Seminar at Middle School
Social	Meet with my mastermind group
Technology	Complete computer programming course

Remember our quote at the beginning of this section. Focus on your potential, not your limitations. Focus on progress, not perfection. Everyone is at different stages of life. Not everyone can be as disciplined as Paul. It took him a long time to develop this discipline. Remember, don't make your expectations too high. In time, these steps will become easier.

ATTENTION = LOVE

Would you agree that ATTENTION equals LOVE? Let us explain: If you paid attention to your children would they think that you loved them? Well, what if you totally ignored them? Do you think they would feel you loved them? I don't think so. So we must FOCUS and pay attention to the Areas of Life that are most important to us.

Be like a laser and focus on what you love!

Being Present

Just because you choose to spend time with your kids doesn't necessarily mean you are focused on them. Are we on our cell phones, on our computers, watching TV? That's not focusing. To show your kids that you love them, you need to be present. That is why at the start of all Empowered Mastery's programs we always insist that our clients turn their phones off and eliminate all distractions so they can be present and focus.

We want you to focus on your top CORE 4 Areas of Life first. Why four? Well, think of a car. A car has four tires, right? But if one of those tires has a flat what will happen? Maybe the car won't drive as efficiently. What if two or three of those tires had a flat or even a slow leak? The car will drive even slower, that's if it can drive at all.

Most of us only have air in one or two of our tires. We are only focusing in on two Areas of Life. If that is the case, our car (or vehicle of life) will not be as efficient. If you want to drive a car all four of your top Areas of Life must have air in them. Now, some of our clients may not be ready for a car so we only have them begin to ride a bicycle, with two Areas of Life.

When you can handle a bicycle, then a car, maybe you upgrade to having a trailer on your car or even begin to drive one of those tractor-trailer trucks. Just make sure you can drive with air in your tires. Yes, sometimes you may get a flat or even have a slow leak, that's okay, just be smart enough to pull over and fill up with air or buy a new tire!

EXERCISE:

Write your new CORE four areas of life, and three Action Steps to
focus on that will improve that area.

AREA OF LIFE	FOCUSED ACTION STEP
1.	
a.	
b.	
c.	
2.	
a.	
b.	
c.	
3.	
a.	
b.	
c.	
4.	
a.	
b.	
c.	

Schedule your ACTION STEPS.

Have you ever scheduled an important meeting? No matter what, you made sure you blocked out time for that meeting, right? How about a very important client? Someone that's really important? I bet you made sure you were there. Well the same goes for your Action Steps!

You must block out time throughout your day, week and month to focus on your action items.

How did you do with this chapter? Did you find it difficult to focus? Were you able to read through it in one sitting? Reading this chapter itself is a good exercise on focusing. This chapter more than any other should be read over and over again, because with each review you will learn and digest more and more.

CHAPTER SUMMARY

- Focus unleashes trapped creative energy.
- A strong belief along with a positive attitude can help you to overcome illness.
- Self-control increases your ability to focus.
- Self-control helps you to react to situations in a calm manner.
- The scientific act and the art of focusing are absolutely vital to your success.
- Focus on what you want.
- Focus on progress, not perfection.
  * Attention equals love—Be like a laser and focus on Action Steps that will enhance your CORE 4 Areas of Life

CHAPTER SEVEN

Opportunities

> In the middle of difficulty lies opportunity.
> —ALBERT EINSTEIN

Each one of us faces obstacles at some time in our life. None of us are immune. However, it's what you do with those challenges in life that ultimately determine who you become and what you accomplish. Very few people in this world are able to turn obstacles into opportunities. One person could grow up in poverty and come to the realization that they will never be anyone of importance, while another in that same circumstance realizes that's the very reason why they must become important.

The first sees circumstance as a stumbling block that creates impossibility. The second uses the "obstacle" as a way to relate to people that opens doors and leads to success. Same circumstance, completely different outcome. One of the best examples of this is Oprah Winfrey. Having spent her early years in poverty-stricken, rural Mississippi, Winfrey later faced sexual molestation and the death of her child as she aged. Today, the talk-show host is as well known for her generosity as she is for her fame. Funding a $40 million school for girls in Africa is just one of Winfrey's many charitable acts. And the only difference between her and others who grew up in similar poverty was her mindset. The following are other examples of people who turned obstacles into opportunities.

1. Woody Allen. The Academy Award-winning writer/producer/director flunked motion picture production at both New York University and the City College of New York and also failed English at N.Y.U.
2. Lucille Ball was once dismissed from drama school for being too quiet and shy.
3. Quaker Oats, Wrigley's, and Pepsi Cola went bankrupt three times.
4. In 1962, Decca Recording Company turned down the Beatles.
5. In 1876, Alexander Graham Bell offered the exclusive rights of the telephone to Western Union for $100,000. William Orton, Western Union's president, turned down the offer, remarking, "What use could this company make of an electrical toy?"
6. Albert Einstein failed his first college entrance exam at Zurich Polytechnic.
7. Malcolm Forbes, the late editor-in-chief of Forbes magazine, one of the largest business publications in the world, did not make the staff of his university newspaper.
8. Michael Jordan was cut from his high school basketball team.
9. Steve Jobs was fired from the company he created, Apple, only to return as CEO when the company suffered some hard times.
10. Jay-Z couldn't get signed to any record labels.

Fear is the roadblock to opportunities.

Too many people are afraid to move forward. It is almost as if they are scared of success. No sooner do they begin a new endeavor, than they quickly decide they aren't going to succeed. Let's use an analogy of rock climbing.

Most people stand and stare at the huge rock looming over them. They know it will be difficult and at times even scary. So why do they take that first step? Because they know the end result outweighs the trials and tribulations along the way. Those are the ultra-successful individuals who not only surmount the obstacle in their path, they gain the skill and confidence to then climb any mountain they face.

BEFORE YOU CAN TURN AN OBSTACLE INTO AN OPPORTUNITY, LET'S TAKE A FEW STEPS BACKWARD AND COMPLETE THE FOLLOWING CONDITIONING FOR SUCCESS EXERCISES.

List five major decisions you made recently.

1.

2.

3.

4.

5.

Do those decisions serve your goals or work against them?

1.

2.

3.

4.

5.

List five decisions you are currently facing.

1.

2.

3.

4.

5.

" In August of 1993, my wife Linda and I were prepared to give birth to our first-born son, Nicholas. Much to our dismay, Nicholas did not survive. The cord was caught, and he suffocated and died in my arms. This is life's ultimate challenge. The memories of the future were gone. I had to be strong for Linda and for everyone else who was deeply affected by this tragedy, but no one knew the pain that I was feeling. I was like the song, 'Tears of a Clown,' happy on the outside but empty and depressed on the inside. How could I convert this challenge in our lives, the worst possible thing that can happen to a parent, to an opportunity? I began to write a letter to Nicholas:

Dear Nicholas. It has been forty-six days since you left Mommy and me, and I really want you to know how much we miss you. There hasn't been a minute that we don't think about you; your cute little nose, big blue eyes, that pudgy face. You are truly our angel from God. We will miss your first steps, we will miss the first time you say Mommy or Daddy, we will miss your laughter and crying, we will miss the first time you blow out the candle on your first birthday cake, we will miss playing catch with you or taking you to the park, we will miss the memories of the future, we will miss all the rest of our years here on earth with you, but that's okay because we know God's promise, that we will someday be together again.

In the few minutes that we knew you and in the nine months that you were in Mommy's tummy, you've given us more love, more peace, and more joy than we've ever had, and we want to say thank you for that. A great person once told me 'hope touches the intangible, sees the invisible, and achieves the impossible.' We truly believe that hope is God.

How much we long to hold you, to kiss you, and to cuddle with you. Through this emptiness in our lives, we seem to find peace or a fulfillment through the power of God. People say that a son usually walks in the shadow of his father's footsteps, but today we begin our journey walking in the light of our son, a light that shines so brightly and never burns, a light that strengthens us each and every day. Thank you for giving us that light. We miss you, love always, Daddy and Mommy. "

—NICK

It is not the events in life that shape your destiny, but the decisions you make about those events. Becoming aware of them, and consciously and carefully choosing your responses or reactions to those circumstances gives you unlimited power. By just paying attention to the decisions you make on a daily basis and nothing else, you're well on your way to creating the life you desire. This places you firmly on that pedestal with the elite achievers. Circumstance can no longer be the opportunity for an excuse. You have successfully eliminated "obstacles" from your life.

Fortunately and unfortunately, injuries are part of martial arts as well as any physical activity. There are countless stories of setbacks in one's training. It is through the injuries or setbacks that the dedicated practitioner will find the opportunity to work on another technique with another part of the body. For example, if a practitioner injures the right leg, they now have an opportunity to develop and strengthen their left techniques. A challenge that students also have is their inability to relax when executing their motions. When an injury occurs, we recommend to the students that they practice softly and all of a sudden, they are improving their training due to a setback. Now that is an opportunity!

{
Whenever you see a successful business, someone once made a courageous decision.

—PETER F. DRUCKER
}

How Successful People Make Decisions

We all make an infinite number of mundane decisions every day—from what we are going to eat to what we are going to watch on TV to all of the decisions we make at work. Most of the major decisions we make, however, are based on our Paradigms. We might vote for one party due to how our parents voted. The same goes for our investing. Where we live, the jobs we take, and even how we bring up our children involves how we were taught. When we struggle with these decisions, it can be the start of major conflict.

Deciding not to make a decision at all is what usually separates the average from the successful. Indecision sets up an internal conflict within ourselves, which in turn brings about all the stress we have in our lives. At some points, we might face a decision with ambivalence, which is defined as opposed feelings toward the same objective. For example, should we eat at this restaurant or that one? Or should I work out or put it off till tomorrow?

Successful people make numerous major decisions on a daily basis. They make them quickly and change them very slowly if at all. Below are the ABCD's of successful decision-making.

A. Assume Risks—All successful people assume risks when making decisions. This is what decision making is all about.

B. Burden Lifted—When you make a decision, you will find that a tremendous burden is lifted from your shoulders and you are happier for it. It also frees your mind to move on and tackle the next decision.

C. Courage & Commitment—Decision-making means having the courage and conviction to make them. President Roosevelt said it best, "The buck stops here." A successful person has the commitment to stand by that decision no matter what the obstacle. President Reagan said, "When I've gathered enough information to make a decision, I don't take a vote, I make a decision." Have enough courage and confidence to believe your decision is the best and commit to its result.

D. Direction toward Your Worthy Ideal—A decision must put you on a path of right direction that is in alignment with your Worthy Ideal. This will then funnel down to your goals which will have substantial meaning because they are related to your Worthy Ideal. Your decision must be in sync with your Worthy Ideals.

Most people make decisions after they have found the resources to do so.

This is perhaps the most common and unfortunately the biggest mistake you can make. If you wait to find the resources, then you might never find them and if you do, it probably will be too late and the opportunity will have already passed you by. We believe that the hardest part of making a decision is making the decision. Once you have overcome that obstacle, the opportunities will then present themselves.

Make your decision first and the resources will follow. History is filled with successful people who had this in common. The decisions they made were in tune with their Worthy Ideal. They were committed to it despite everyone's limiting beliefs and they made the decision before they found the resources. Did Thomas Edison have the resources to invent the light bulb before he made the decision to experiment in his lab? No, and yet he made the decision to do so and committed to it despite failing an astounding ten thousand times. By the way, Thomas Edison didn't believe he failed; he felt he'd created ten thousand ways not to make a light bulb. Below are a few more examples of people who chose to make their decision without having the needed resources.

1. Sir Edmund Hillary—He was the first person to successfully climb Mt. Everest. He made the decision to start on his journey before there was any blueprint on how to do it.
2. Roger Bannister—He was the first person to run a four-minute mile when it was thought to be impossible. Medical experts stated that our bodies weren't capable of withstanding the stress, yet he made the decision before he had the resources.
3. Lillian Vernon—Lillian Vernon became a household name at a time when women were not even supposed to work outside the home. She started a business in the kitchen of her small home and grew it to be one of the most well-known, multi-million dollar companies in the United States as well as the first female-owned company to be listed on the American Stock Exchange. Today, she continues to be one of the country's leading catalog retailers.

When you make a decision and commit to it the resources will come to you.

“ I was set to close on my commercial building on Tuesday, January 15. I needed $75,000 for the down payment. It was Friday evening, January 11, and I had just received word that my private funding wasn't going to come through. To make matters worse, it was a holiday weekend, the banks were closed, and I wasn't anywhere close to having the money. I took a step back, took a deep breath, and said, 'I can do this.' I called my wife and one of my top instructors into my office and said these exact words. 'We have a situation; the money we were going to get just fell through. We need to come up with $75K by Tuesday or we lose the deal. I know every reason in the world why we can't make this happen, and I don't want to hear any of them. All I want to know is how we are going to make this work.' After about an hour of brainstorming, my wife, Kathy, Master G. and I decided to sell lifetime memberships to my students. They would pay a certain amount of money up front and could then come to any of the programs we offer for as long as they liked. They would never have to pay tuition again. We also set up a program so that if a student advanced any amount of tuition, then we would double it on the back end of the membership. We e-mailed all of our students and the response was great. We sold a number of lifetime memberships, and many students took us up on our offer. We did fall short of raising the $75,000. However, in three days over the holiday weekend and thanks to my wife spending hours and hours on the phone, we managed to raise $74, 989.11. We managed to find the remaining $10.89. We were able to close on the property and continued to fulfill a lifelong dream of owning our own martial arts building. ”

—CHRIS

When a problem occurs, you often hear that you need to "get past" it or avoid it. This is not true; you first need to see it as a challenge. This is vital in so many ways. How do you feel when you have a problem: stressed, anxious, and fearful? How do you feel when you face a challenge: excited, inspired, and energized? See the difference? The next step is to learn to transform your challenges into opportunities. By following this process, you are enhancing your chances for success. When you encounter a challenge or an obstacle, how do you react? Most successful people embrace challenges and look at them as opportunities to grow. There are three levels of language to convert obstacles to opportunities. The levels include:

1. Level One. "I have a problem." or "There is a problem." "Problem" is another word that should be permanently eliminated from your vocabulary. Problems just don't exist in the world of Empowered Mastery.
2. Level Two. "I have a challenge." or "I'm excited to find a solution for this challenge."
3. Level Three. "This is a great opportunity." or "How is this an opportunity?" or "What's good about this?" or "How can I learn from this?"

Some of the greatest inventions, from penicillin to Post-It Notes, came from visionary people who chose not to "get past" or avoid the obstacle, but rather to turn it into an opportunity. In 1968, a researcher at 3M was researching the development of an extremely strong adhesive. One of his batches of glue was very weak, hardly strong enough to hold two pieces of paper together. Rather than toss it out, he discussed it with his colleagues. Later, another 3M researcher, Art Fry, sat in his church choir struggling to keep paper bookmarks from falling out of his hymnal. He remembered the weak glue and wondered if it had the ability to re-adhere once pulled loose. Using the failed glue, Fry began experimenting; Post-it Notes were the ultimate result. They are now one of 3M's most profitable products.

Pain can be turned into gain, a problem can be turned into a profit, and an obstacle can become a glorious opportunity. Here are seven ways you can turn an obstacle into an opportunity.

1. Seek out the advantage inside the adversity.
2. Keep obstacles in perspective.
3. Identify new opportunities.
4. Ask for help.
5. Accept responsibility.
6. Be persistent.
7. Learn to laugh at yourself.

There is good in everything.

The best life lessons come when we are challenged and pushed to the edge. Adversity is often the preamble to greater achievement. Adversity reveals true character. Those who face personal trials either rise to the occasion or fall down in despair. A crisis strips away all pretenses and reveals true character. Are you the sort that feels beaten down by the obstacles in your life, or do you use them and profit from your challenges? Take any successful person you know and you will find that they faced obstacles. They used the difficulty to their advantage. All successful people experience failure at some point, however, turning these failures into achievements are true signs of success. Remember the examples of the famous people we spoke about above.

Everybody makes mistakes, blunders, and errors of judgment. The key for successful and vital living lies in the way we respond to those human shortcomings. Most successful people view mistakes as learning experiences and rarely make the same one twice. Consider these ways of responding to your mistakes so that those mistakes work for you rather than against you.

1. Choose to admit the mistake. Those who stop making excuses are always the ones who start making results. When it's obvious that you have erred, acknowledge it to yourself and to others who may be affected. Doing so allows you to take ownership of the situation and begin the process of correcting and adjusting.

2. Choose to act. Perhaps the biggest mistake when making a mistake lies in not changing directions. Don't let an error in judgment preclude you from taking corrective action. Remember that life rewards action.

3. Choose to apologize. Promptly and honestly say the right words when the wrong things have happened.

4. Choose to learn from the mistake. Every mistake contains within it a tremendous opportunity for learning and growth. When you make a mistake, don't ignore it.

Below is a great Conditioning for Success Exercise to help you transform an obstacle into an opportunity. As an example, we've used the story of Chris and his financial challenge while purchasing his building from earlier. Fill in your own challenges and create a corresponding opportunity for each. When doing this exercise, remember the Law of Polarity. The Law of Polarity states that everything in the universe has an opposite and cannot exist otherwise. If there is an up, there has to be a down. If there is a left, there has to be a right. If something appears to be a challenge, then there has to be an opportunity as well.

CHALLENGE	OPPORTUNITY
$75,000 in three days	Create lifetime memberships

1.

2.

3.

4.

5.

6.

7.

8.

9.

10.

CHAPTER SUMMARY

- There are no problems—just challenges.
- No negative event or circumstance should prevent you from achieving your goals.
- Stop focusing on obstacles. Instead focus on how they can be of benefit to you.
- Conquering your challenges paves the road to success.
- Make the decision to act and the resources will follow.
- Adversity reveals your true character.
- Mistakes are inevitable. Successful people respond to mistakes as learning experiences.

CHAPTER EIGHT

Realization

> Are you bored with life? Then throw yourself into some new work you believe in with all your heart, live for it, die for it, and you will find happiness that you thought never could be yours.
>
> **—DALE CARNEGIE**

At one point or another in your life, you might take a deep look inside and come to the realization that you aren't fulfilled. It is important to understand that the realization of your purpose is the number one priority. Before you can live according to it, you have to know what it is. At times, it is difficult to concentrate because there are many situations and circumstances in life that make focusing on your purpose challenging.

These difficult times are when you need to keep a stable mind and look toward the future. Every day is a test to see if you have come to this realization. Throughout this chapter, we'll talk about discovering your Life's Purpose and living according to your Worthy Ideal. Realization is the act of knowing what you want out of life and working to achieve it. Later in this chapter we ask you to define your Life's Purpose. Refer to the illustration below, and to chapter 3, where we discuss your Worthy Ideal.

Worthy Ideal and Life's Purpose

Whatever you are passionate about guides you to your Worthy Ideal. So many times in our seminars we hear participants say, "I don't have a Worthy Ideal." Or "I don't have a Life's Purpose." Some people may be confused with the differences between a Worthy Ideal and Life's Purpose.

WORTHY IDEAL	LIFE'S PURPOSE
WHY we do what we do.	HOW we do what we do.
Bigger than you.	About you.

Empowered Mastery's Worthy Ideal is to inspire and impact professionals and entrepreneurs to achieve ULTIMATE success personally, professionally, spiritually and physically so they can live a life filled with passion and purpose.

Empowered Mastery's Purpose is to be the best leaders, coaches and teachers we can be for our family, friends and clients. We will do this by incorporating EMC's principals and philosophies into all aspects of our lives. Everything we do each and every day is to work together with you for this one purpose.

Our Worthy Ideal is why we do what we do. Our purpose explains how we do it. You can't fulfill your Life's Purpose unless you have a Worthy Ideal. Your Worthy Ideal is what drives you to get out of bed in the morning. Oftentimes we also hear in our seminars that people equate their Life's Purpose with money. This isn't the case. Money is just a means to a lifestyle. Everyone has purpose.

Once you realize your purpose, you can't ignore it. It is just a matter of discovery. Some people find theirs right away while they are young, others not until they get older. There is no age requirement or expiration date on realizing your purpose. It is never too late to realize yours.

Every once in a while we meet someone who inspires us. These people exude enthusiasm and care genuinely about what they're doing, who they work with, and who they surround themselves with. They express a joy from deep within; it's not forced or superficial. You sense their true passion and selflessness. They also have a genuine care toward those around them because they've come to the realization and fulfillment of their Life's Purpose. Because of this realization, they are consciously and continuously working on purpose. They live according to their Worthy Ideal and know the difference they want to make.

Once you come to this realization as well, your work will be consistent with your purpose. Clarity and focus on purpose sets us apart from most of the people in this world. Who has come to this realization? It can be anyone—a teacher, parent, or someone you just met. It doesn't matter who they are, where they come from, or what they do. What matters is that they've accepted this realization. Their purpose echoes through their actions.

Fulfillment comes from the inside out, not vice versa. Take a minute and think of the people in your life who seem to love what they do. In the space provided, write down the names of three people who know their Life's Purpose and describe the characteristics and qualities they possess.

PEOPLE WHO HAVE A PURPOSE IN LIFE

	NAME	CHARACTERISTIC
1.		
2.		
3.		

Many times the word passion is used to describe purpose. In Chapter 3, we defined the difference between the two. Passion isn't intellectual or rational. Instead it stems from the heart.

> 66 In my previous business, I had tremendous success yet wasn't happy. I had no direction, drive, or purpose. Fortunately, I was able to retire at age thirty-nine. To everyone on the outside, my life appeared perfect. On the inside, however, I was still unhappy. I sat home, watched movies, slept, and ate. I became lazy and irritable. I was like Michael Keaton in the movie Mr. Mom. I rarely shaved and my daily attire was sweats and an old flannel shirt. I was envious of those around me who woke up each morning with a purpose and went to bed each night fulfilled with a sense of accomplishment. What I was missing was the realization of a Worthy Ideal and my Life's Purpose. In the end, it took me forty-seven years to finally realize what I am truly passionate about. I have found both my Worthy Ideal in forming Empowered Mastery and also the forum to fulfill my Life's Purpose by speaking to schools, corporations, and other organizations to help others live fulfilled lives. 99
>
> —RICK

If we fail to listen to our purpose in life, we experience stress, fatigue, frustration, and dissatisfaction.

Worthy Ideal ➝ Life's Purpose ➝ Transform your life

Think of what type of person you have to become in order to fulfill your Worthy Ideal.

Some people may be confused with a Life Purpose and Worthy Ideal.

Before you can do something, you must first be something.

—GOETHE

A Life Purpose is a model for the person YOU ultimately want to BECOME within your lifetime. The primary target is the word BECOME. Most people are always focused on what they want to do, where they want to go, and what they want to have.

That mindset is working from the outside in not the inside out. To us that is backward. Everything in the universe grows from the inside out not the outside in. So in order for you to have the things you want; money, relationships, house, car, job, or physical body, you must first become a certain type of person inside.

The "having" mode is certainly seductive. But by definition having is possessing, and that means it can disappear as easily as it came. We are born with nothing and leave this world with nothing as well. People remember who you are, not what you possessed. The "being" mode is the most important.

In this state, you are centered, authentic, and connected to your spiritual self. You have your personal power to assist you in creating and realizing your Life Purpose. If you can comfortably be yourself (without living from your "shoulds"), then your need for outside approval disappears.

Becoming the person you want to be is the primary target. This is your first focus.

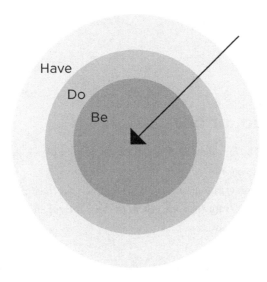

For the aspiring martial artist, there comes a point in time where you come to the realization of who you are. We teach many dedicated adults and teenagers to learn the skills to instruct. Watching teenagers excel in instructing and making a huge positive difference in the children that they teach is nothing less than amazing. Where many teenagers are going out smoking, drinking and doing other less desirable acts; our Junior Instructors are changing the lives of others. They have accepted and realized the responsibilities that come with being an instructor, and it is that identity that then funnels through the other areas of their life. This sense of responsibility informs their life both inside and outside of the martial arts school. That is how we make leaders in the martial arts.

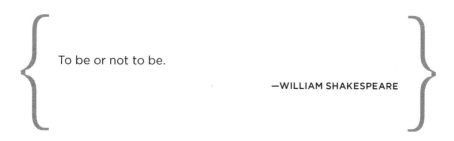

To be or not to be.

—WILLIAM SHAKESPEARE

To have, do, or be?

In the book *To Have or to Be?* Eric Fromm described a group of people living their lives trying to:

- Have enough (money, resources, things) so that they can. . .
- Do what they want (in terms of work, how they spend their time), because then they can. . .
- Be happy.

This group made the common mistake of thinking from the outside in. Fulfilled people want to first be happy and then do and have the things they desire. This is thinking from the inside out.

EXERCISE:

What are certain "BE" qualities that you think you need to incorporate into your identity or character that will support your Worthy Ideal and Life's Purpose?

I want to BE: _____

_____

I want to BE: _____

_____

I want to BE: _____

_____

I want to BE: _____

_____

I want to BE: _____

_____

As you write down all the "BE" qualities that you would like to possess as a person, they can be qualities or characteristics that you currently have or that you would like to have within your lifetime. For example:

I want to be passionate, dedicated, confident, focused, considerate etc.

Unfortunately, most people get stuck at the first step. This is because they're trying to live their life from the outside in rather than the inside out. They can never have enough. This is why 'BE' is at the center of the main target. One day you reach the end of your life and realize you've never accomplished anything. In order for you to have a fulfilling life you must think from the inside out:

- Be who you are. Know your strengths, weaknesses, and your Worthy Ideal and Life's Purpose. This self-awareness will lead you to. . .
- Do what you love. This doing will be the contribution of your unique gifts. Because you are giving yourself away, you will be rewarded, and. . .
- Have what you need. Of course, there are no guarantees you will have everything you want!

So, how do we do this? First, making money must cease to be our primary goal.

Stop measuring success by your bank account and possessions. Get your priorities in order and follow your heart, as guided by your Worthy Ideal and Life's Purpose.

The "having" mode is certainly seductive. But by definition having is possessing, and that means it can disappear as easily as it came. We are born with nothing and leave this world with nothing. People remember who you are, not what you possessed. The "being" mode is not so transient. In this state, you are centered, authentic, and connected to your spiritual self. You have your personal power to assist you in creating and realizing your purpose. If you can comfortably be yourself (without living from your "shoulds"), then your need for outside approval disappears.

From the centered place of "being," your vision of who you are can express itself. You will be drawn to your purpose. In the "having" mode, you feel driven. It is no coincidence that you hear about being "market-driven" or even "value-driven." These concepts come out of the "having" mode. The language of purpose is "value-led" or "customer-led." What feels better to you, being led, or being driven?

Think back over times when you have felt inspired—times when you were drawn to a person or an idea. Recall situations in which you thought to yourself, "I'd like to make that kind of impact." When you felt inspired you may have noticed that you reacted physically with shivers up your spine, or with tears of awe. Describe three situations when you felt inspired.

1.

2.

3.

As you reflect on those situations did you feel pulled to take any action? Your purpose will be an inspiration to you if you let it be.

> It's true that we don't know what we've got until we lose it, but it's also true that we don't know what we've been missing until it arrives.
>
> **—ANONYMOUS**

Qualities of being

We spend so much of our time doing or having that sometimes it is difficult to understand what it means to be. The following Conditioning for Success Exercise should help. Review the following list of "being" qualities. Place an X beside the ones you have experienced. Put a Y beside the qualities you would like to develop. For example, we've listed a few of our own; please add any to the list that you feel are important.

1. Discipline ☐
2. Responsibility ☐
3. Positive Self-Image ☐

4. Being Present ☐
5. Awareness ☐
6. Vision ☐
7. ☐
8. ☐
9. ☐
10. ☐

> You never find yourself until you face the truth.
>
> —PEARL BAILEY

Who Are You?
I am positive. I am focused.
I am energetic. I am healthy.
I am loving. I am patient.
I am grateful.
I am rich and abundant.

—NICK

In previous chapters, we talked about Muhammad Ali. Most people think he adopted the mantra "I am the greatest" after he became a successful boxer. In fact, he said it before he even knew he was. None of us have the power to read the future. But we do have belief in ourselves, and the knowledge that greatness is inside us. In Chapter 5, we asked you to write down your "I AM" affirmations. We feel these statements are so important that now that you have this new information, we want you to write them again. In the following Conditioning Exercise, answer this question ten times. Add any of the "BE" qualities from the previous exercise and convert them into "I AM" statements. Just write, don't think about your answer.

"I AM" STATEMENTS

1. I AM...

2. I AM...

3. I AM...

4. I AM...

5. I AM...

6. I AM...

7. I AM...

8. I AM...

9. I AM...

10. I AM...

> The purpose of life is a life of purpose.
>
> —ROBERT BYRNE

Why is this Your Worthy Ideal/Life Purpose?

In Chapter 3, we asked you to write your Worthy Ideal. Now go back and review what you wrote. With the information you've learned in this chapter, make any improvements and rewrite your Worthy Ideal. Write out your Life's Purpose as you now understand it in the box below. You might want to include the following parts in your statement: first, use a verb to describe your purpose (serve, teach, train, write, create, counsel, make, sell). Then choose a noun to describe who or what (children, the elderly, consumers, the earth, the poor, computers). Also include the skill and talents you will use. Finally, include the outcome that you want.

So let's begin writing your Life's Purpose Statement.

Your Life Purpose Statement Must Have The Following:

1. Be stated in the positive.
2. Have "Be" and "Do" statements.
3. Include yourself and others.
4. Should be able to be experienced every day.
5. Eliminate Universals (always, never, everyone, etc.).
6. Use emotionally "charged" words that resonate with you.
7. Remember, this statement must make you happy...*really* happy.

Use the template below as a guide.

Feel free to change and customize what resonates with you.

The purpose of my life is to be the best _____,

_____, _____ I can be.

To enjoy a life of _____, _____,

_____, _____.

I do this by _____, _____,

_____, _____.

For myself _____, _____,

_____, _____.

> 66 The purpose of my life is to be an inspirational leader, and to enjoy a healthy, vital life of love, gratitude, passion, contribution, and financial abundance. I will do this by living my life to its full potential, leading by example and sharing my specialized knowledge. For myself, for my family, and the students I teach. 99
>
> —PAUL

IMPROVED WORTHY IDEAL:

LIFE'S PURPOSE:

Empowered Mastery's Purpose *is to be the best leaders, coaches and teachers we can be for our family, friends and clients. We will do this by incorporating EMC's principals and philosophies into all aspects of our lives.*

> Our life is composed greatly from dreams, from the unconscious, and they must be brought into connection with action. They must be woven together.
>
> **—ANAÏS NIN**

Fulfilling your purpose

You may have thought of your purpose as some grand endeavor that seemed difficult to accomplish. But now you can actually see on paper how you have already been living it, even if through small actions. Now increase those actions each week. For example, if a part of your Life's Purpose is to be a good parent, what do you need to do to fulfill that Purpose? Read to your kids, spend quality time with them, and teach them the difference between right and wrong. Before you know it, you will have raised them correctly and sent them out into the world as a good finder.

No feat is too big to accomplish as long as you apply your talents along with your intellectual qualities. You soon will live a life once thought unimaginable. Everyone is capable of achieving greatness, but only those with a defined purpose and clear vision will realize success in life. Realization gives you an insight into the future and an image of where your purpose and vision will be five or ten years from now. If you want to live a purposeful life, then you are going to have to take action and make it a reality. Your life cannot propel forward unless you provide the initial push. If you aren't growing, you're dying.

CHAPTER SUMMARY

- Before you can live your Life's Purpose, you must first realize and find your Worthy Ideal.
- Your Life's Purpose is how you want to be remembered as a person.
- Live in the "be" mode of life.
- You will be remembered for who you are and not for your material possessions.
- Review your actions in life. Do they support your Worthy Ideal? Do they enable you to live according to your Life's Purpose?

CHAPTER NINE

Meditation

{
Meditation brings wisdom; lack of meditation leaves ignorance. Know well what leads you forward and what holds you back, and choose the path that leads to wisdom.

—BUDDHA
}

We often begin our meditation seminars for both companies and schools with this quote, "Life creates it, makes it grow. Its energy surrounds us and binds us. Luminious beings are we, not this crude matter. You must feel the [energy] around you, here, between you, me, the tree, the rock, everywhere, yes."

Do you know who said this? When we ask our seminar participants, the answers range from Plato and Socrates to Thomas Edison and Martin Luther King. When we tell them it's Master Yoda from The Empire Strikes Back, they are shocked. We have to admit that we do change the word "force" to "energy" so as not to give it away. George Lucas researched Eastern philosophy for years to develop the concept of the "Force" in the Star Wars universe. Now, we're not going to teach you to lift X-wing fighters out of a swamp, but we can teach you how to tap into this higher energy source that Eastern philosophers have been practicing for thousands of years.

Here's another question first: do you believe in a higher power? If so, how do you tap into that higher power and energize your life? For the majority of people, this is too much to grasp. Most people would agree that everything is energy. If you take any physical item and look through a sufficiently powerful microscope, you will see that everything is a molecular structure vibrating at a particular rate—the denser the item, the faster the vibration, and the more tightly compacted the molecular structure. Let's take water for example.

Water provides a great analogy for explaining how we have the ability to tap into a higher power. In a physical state, a person is able to see, touch, taste, hear, and smell water. The water is in a physical form and vibrates at a particular rate. We call this a corporeal vibration. Once water boils at 212° Fahrenheit, it turns to steam and becomes a vapor. You can actually hear the molecules vibrating faster as you boil the water. When it is vibrating at a higher rate, you can see the water, yet you don't. It becomes transparent but still visible. The vapor is easily felt, touched, and smelled as well. As you boil it further, the molecules continue to go faster and to vibrate at an etheric level. This same water turns into a gas. You cannot see it or feel it but you still know it exists. In this state, it is impossible to detect water with any of our senses, but we still know it's there. The same is true with our own being. When we are thinking thoughts based on what we see, hear, touch, smell, and taste, we are basing our information on a particular vibration. We are neither here nor there, we just are. In this state, there is no particular enthusiasm or excitement in anything that we do or say. This is a very primitive and animalistic way of thinking.

We are vibrating at a slow vibration. Now, imagine that you start to get excited about something. Perhaps someone gave you an idea about a new business venture, an exercise regimen you feel confident you can follow, or you have decided to go on a weeklong vacation to the Caribbean. The idea came in, you become emotionally attached, and suddenly you start to theorize on how this new idea could be made to work. You start to visualize and use your IQ's to formulate desired results that don't exist yet, except in your mind. This is like the steam you can still see and touch. The idea exists in your mind but it is not tangible at this time. A fire now burns inside of you, creating a higher vibration, and you start to think of solutions to obtain the desired result, as if turning up a flame to boil water. Now, for a select few, the new idea that has been formulated in your mind then comes to fruition through a power far beyond your own physical capacity.

There is a power that flows to and through you that provides epiphanies or solutions to obtain the results you are searching for.

At this point, you are vibrating at a very high frequency, tapping into an energy that you definitely cannot see. This is what sets apart the best from the rest, their ability to tap into a higher power and live on a plane that most people only dream of. It can only happen if you are emotionally connected to the Worthy Ideal that you are working toward. The beauty of this is that while few people have the ability to do this, we can show you how. Meditation is the pathway to help you tap into a spiritual power that you never knew you had.

Your higher power is lying inside of your subconscious right now. Most of us have a thousand ideas running through our mind. These are the thoughts of your conscious mind, and as long as they are there you will not get in touch with your subconscious. The key is to relax and let those thoughts go. True relaxation—the kind that relieves you of all your daily pressure, stresses, and obligations—revitalizes you. We all have a tremendous amount of potential energy inside of us, but most of us don't know how to tap into that force. Instead, we remain sluggish. Meditation is one of the best methods to tap into those unlimited amounts of energy. When we energize ourselves, we are better suited for finding our purpose and living our vision.

Many feel that meditation is only for the "gurus" and people who sit "Indian style" with palms up, eyes closed and humming. Despite what you might have been told or saw or thought with your five senses, meditation is more common than you might think.

Would you believe it if we told you that you have probably been practicing meditation for a long time? Let's prove it by asking this question: do you participate in a recreational activity that you love? It might be running, hiking, or perhaps you like to walk around the block in your neighborhood. It could even be an exercise regimen, like bike riding or an even more intense activity like skiing or snowboarding. Or something more relaxed like reading, listening to music, or doing a craft. If it's an activity that you enjoy completely and that engulfs your mind to the point where you are able to be free from all other thoughts, then you are practicing meditation.

We believe that meditation is a single activity that engulfs your mind, body, and spirit, all in one. This is done by having the ability to free your mind of unwanted thoughts while gaining the ability to focus on one thing. A time when you are completely in sync with whatever you are doing at a moment is indeed a form of meditation.

Did you ever notice that when you are completely engulfed in an activity and free from other thoughts that you will come up with unbelievable ideas. Sometimes, those ideas could be life changing. This is because you have tapped into a higher frequency or faster vibration than the physical. Your body was one with the activity, which allowed the thought power, or energy, to flow to and through you by coming up with epiphany-like ideas.

Another example comes from a question we ask at our seminars: "Where do you get your best ideas?" The answers vary but a majority of the time someone always says either while driving or taking a shower. Why is this? Because during both of these activities, you are relaxed and extremely comfortable, which allows thoughts to come and go freely.

Now on the contrary how many thoughts come to you freely when you are in a stressful traffic situation? None, because energy cannot flow freely when you are stressed. That is why it is crucial to practice some form of meditation that allows our minds to be free and relaxed. Let's put this another way, with water again. Imagine there's a hose and water is flowing freely through it. This is very similar to how Ki (Life Source) energy flows through us. A stressful situation is like kinking the hose so the water only trickles out. Energy does not and will not ever flow in stressful situations; it is a blockage in your system that restricts your internal energy system. Meditation will allow your thought energy to flow to and through you helping you find solutions to your challenges and answers to your questions. The results will be astounding.

Now that you understand you have already been practicing some form of meditation, let's dive into more "traditional" methods, which will allow your thought power to increase and give you the results you desire.

For us the best way to combat the unwanted side effects of a hectic life is to understand the concept of meditation. The best times to meditate are as soon as you get up in the morning and right before you go to bed in the evening. Your subconscious mind is more susceptible to impact during these times. Meditation is not as detailed or challenging as many think. The ultimate goal is to lower your resistance and come into alignment with your own source of energy, and to raise your spiritual level. When you're able to put yourself in a relaxed position and quiet your mind, then you stop that resistance and tap into a higher energy source. Meditation is an art, in that you must get better at not thinking and quieting your mind.

As martial arts practitioners, masters, and professionals we have had the honor and privilege to learn about meditation from one of the most spiritual people we know, Grand Master Byung Min Kim. He is not only a martial arts grand master but also our spiritual mentor and guide in our quest for enlightenment. He has the honor of training with his master, who has helped him achieve great success in the area of meditation while traveling on the path to spiritual enlightenment. We've been taught many different styles of meditation including:

- Concentration meditation. In this type, you focus on one item—the flame on a candle, for example.
- Reflective meditation. This is when you return to a past experience and replay it to correct a mistake.
- Visual meditation. In this meditation, you focus only on what you want.
- Self-mastery meditation. This type of meditation is often used when an injury has occurred. In this instance, you visualize yourself channeling Ki energy to the specific area that is injured.

66 The meditation we use, however, is used by our mentor Grand Master Kim and focuses strictly on breathing. When you focus on your breathing and nothing else, your mind clears of all thought. Once this happens, your mind is open and you're able to tap into higher power and creativity. In our experience, this is the best method of meditation. 99

—PAUL & CHRIS

Meditation relaxes our mind and body so energy flows to and through us and opens the doors to a higher power. Setting aside time to practice relaxation and meditation is essential to eliminating the unwanted distractions in your life. Energy won't flow through a restricted environment. Stress, anxiety, fear, and doubt close the pathways for energy. Calmness, love, peace, and gratitude open that pathway.

What makes one of two individuals with the same training and skill surpass the other? What makes two individuals from the same background and education have such different results? Why are some people wealthy and some poor? The difference revolves around who has the ability to tap into a higher power. In professional sports, there is something known as the "zone." This is a time when the athlete is at the top of his game and something special has come over them. Have you ever been in the zone, when everything just flows and happens with minimal effort? Reggie Miller is a good example of this. In 1995, he single-handedly knocked the New York Knicks out of the NBA playoffs by scoring eight points in eleven seconds. In an interview after the game, he remarked that the basket felt like it was eight feet wide and he just couldn't miss. There was something present beyond him that caused events to go as they did. This is what happens when you're in the zone.

The eastern philosophy Taoism promotes calmness and meditation. The Tao is a time in your life when you've completely tapped into that higher power and your body becomes nothing more than a vehicle for whatever the venue is. Reggie Miller was one with the Tao. A good question to ask is "Was there ever a time in my life when I was doing something and everything just went right?"

> 66 I remember when I was fighting against the National champion at the time at the US Team Trials in 1989. He did a technique, and I responded, but I had no clue what had happened. I scored the point and took a hop back and remember thinking, "Holy cow, I just did that," knowing that I had not done it consciously. It just happened. I attribute this to tapping into a higher power. 99
>
> —CHRIS

In the space below, describe a time in your life when you were 'in the zone' and everything went smoothly.

Relaxation techniques nourish you on a deep plane so that you can achieve a higher level of mind-body-spirit awareness. You'll find it's a great way to achieve calmness and serenity. The object is to relax your entire body. Begin by repeating slowly and softly the following four words: calm...peaceful... tranquil...relaxed...

When we are living day to day, we live on the physical plane, all the while obtaining our information from our five senses. When we get motivated, ideas flood our minds. This inspiration unites us with our Worthy Ideal. This is possible to achieve if allow energy to flow to and through you. Professional athletes along with martial artists practice by visualizing events in advance, so by the time they perform, they have already gone through it hundreds of time in their mind and are able to give their best performance.

Think of a future event in your life. Visualize this event, replaying the successful outcome over and over.

66 I have used advanced visualization techniques for competitions and for my black belt promotion levels in Taekwondo. When I graduated to fifth degree, I had already gone through everything mentally way ahead of time so that when I performed, it was as if I had already done every single kick, form, cement breaking, and even knew what the room would look like. 99

—CHRIS

66 The best stress reliever that I've found is meditation. That's what I do to start every day. It's a discipline and a setting of priorities. I'm not going to allow my mind to create situations, expectations, and attitudes that may or may not be true but can negatively influence my experience of the day ahead. Instead, I want to be led by the feeling or the spirit of whatever the reality is and however it manifests. 99

—PHIL JACKSON, 11 NBA TITLES AS A COACH

Most people have a pre-conceived notion that martial arts training is about kicking, punching, fighting, and even cage fighting. They think it is a very physical art. Just the contrary. Martial Arts training is the development of your self physically, mentally and spiritually so one can live a life of health and happiness. A martial artist develops physically through repetition of physical motions, mentally by developing the confidence through their successes and spiritually through meditation. You could only go so far in your training without your spiritual development. There is a point when it goes beyond physical development. When one practices diligently in their meditation, a whole new level of training and deepening understanding presents itself at the perfect moment. When applied properly, your mind, body and spirit work as one and you personally become masterful. At this point you accomplish things in and out of your training that you had previously only dreamed of.

Breathing

The key to meditating is breathing. It is your natural resource to health and:

- Increases your oxygen and blood circulation
- Strengthens your internal organs
- Improves your digestive system
- Builds your immune system
- Balances your hormones
- Quiets your nervous system
- Calms your mind
- Increases your energy level

Breathing is the single most important need that your body requires to function. Breathing is more important than sleeping, eating, or drinking. Breathing and meditation go hand-in-hand. It is vital for the development of your internal energy. In martial arts we call it your Ki energy. Remember, everything grows from the inside out, not the outside in.

Breathing helps overcome almost every challenge. Most of us don't realize that relaxed breathing helps control our emotions, reduce stress, quiet our body, and focus on our thoughts—all things that we want to cultivate and weave throughout every aspect of our lives. Meditation gives us the ability to do that. When we teach meditation, we first focus on our breathing. We inhale and exhale through our nose, bringing the air all the way down to our lower energy center. That inhale breath has to go down low. Most people when they breathe fill up their lungs and their stomach retracts. That is incorrect. When you inhale, the oxygen comes along with positive energy, thoughts, and clean air in and pushes out your lower stomach so it fills up with air. On the exhale, the stomach goes in, and the negative thoughts, doubts, fears, and toxins release from your body. Have you ever watched a baby sleep? Watch their stomach, how it rises with each inhale, and lowers with each exhale. They are born breathing correctly. As we grow, our breathing changes to an improper form. People breathe from their upper chest instead of their lower center.

Every breath has a count to it. If you inhale and exhale once, that is a count. One ten-minute meditation involves counting approximately from one to twenty and back from twenty to one. As you become more comfortable with the meditation, increase the count. From one to fifty and back from fifty to one is about a fifteen-minute meditation; one to one hundred and back is about half an hour. When you are able to do this, ideas will roll in and roll out. Your job is not to resist them but to allow those thoughts to take their natural course. Eventually, when you are in a very relaxed state, the thoughts that come will start to formulate the solutions you are searching for. Why? Because you are letting energy flow to and through you without stress or restriction. A better way to explain this is that our energy in our body is like a hose. When the hose is clear, the water flows easily and effortlessly. When there is a kink in the hose, then the water trickles.

Stress is like a kink in our hose, and the energy cannot flow. Energy stops when we tense or tighten up. In our martial arts training, we practice relaxing completely while we are executing a technique and then snap into a particular position at the end for an explosive impact. Our energy is flowing through us until we choose to abruptly stop the flow onto the target. We cannot get the power in the technique if we first don't completely relax.

Stress breaks a chain if all the pressure is on one link, but when the stress is spread out evenly over the length of the chain then there's no pressure. Meditation helps alleviate that pressure on our chain! If you're tense and stressed, breathing can return your body to a normal level. If you are facing an important decision, stop and breathe. Whenever you have a question in your mind about what to do next or how to do it, breathe. Breathing is the most crucial element of strong emotional and spiritual health.

How you feel is reflected in how you breathe.

Tension and stress have an impact on breathing. Anxiety creates shallow, ineffective breathing, and in stressful situations some people actually hold their breath. Breathing is the foundation of relaxation techniques and meditation. As you breathe, you begin to feel your body relax and almost slow down to match the pace of your breathing. With your total concentration on slow, calm breathing, your muscles will loosen, and your mind will clear. You will not be able to concentrate on challenges, obstacles, or other events in your life if you're totally concentrating on your breathing.

Imagine all of the stress and anxiety in your body being released through this exercise. Visualize the unwanted stress leaving your body and progressing up through your body, first through your toes, then your feet, ankles, calves, knees, thighs, abdomen, lower back, chest, shoulders, arms, wrists, hands, fingers, neck, face, and head. By the time you get to your scalp, you ought to be completely relaxed.

This is all it takes to begin the process of deep, healthy breathing. Allow the fresh oxygen to get down deep into your diaphragm.

Practice your breathing regularly while driving to work in the morning, cooking dinner, and before you go to sleep. With this calming technique perfected, you'll be able to call upon it in times of stress and be better able to handle difficult situations.

It is important to pay attention as you practice your breathing. Let each inhalation empower you, and let go of tension and stress on each exhalation. The rhythm of your breathing sets a calmer pace for your mind and spirit. Clear your mind, if only momentarily, and focus on the sensation of your breathing. Try not to let outside distractions interfere with the process, and definitely try to keep your mind chatter to a minimum and eventually at zero. The ultimate goal is to sharpen your ability to concentrate, to tap into a calmer and more stable state of being, and to be better able to make clearer decisions.

Researchers are beginning to apply scientific measurements to this subjective experience. People who meditate have been found to function more efficiently psychologically. Many of the physiological effects of stress that speed up the aging process are slowed and even, some experts believe, reversed through the process of meditation. One of the most fascinating aspects of this research, which has been ongoing for over two decades, is that long-term meditators can have bodies that are physiologically comparable to typical bodies that are five to twelve years younger.

> 66 Grandmaster Byung Min Kim has the physical appearance of someone twenty years his junior and the physical ability to match. Remember, every seven years, we get a whole new body; why not make the next one your best one. Break free of the paradigm that you are too old, maybe you're just due for a new body. 99
>
> —CHRIS

One of the major results of meditation is a calming of the mind and a deeper level of relaxation. Meditation eases tension, and actually helps you become more accepting of others and, maybe more importantly, accepting of yourself. Meditation teaches you how to enter into a state of relaxation and calmness.

When you first begin to meditate, you should not expect too much too soon. The first day you start studying a foreign language you don't expect to speak it, right? Meditation is simply a way to disentangle us from the clutter and chatter of our minds. Eastern philosophers contend that meditation creates a balance and a flow of energy through the body.

You'll need discipline and practice to achieve the full benefits of meditation. When you meditate, you want to find a comfortable position. Sit against something that supports your back. Your body should be erect while remaining relaxed and comfortable. Finding that steadying posture becomes essential as you practice meditation, so your breath will flow easily throughout the body. It is recommended that you sit crossed-legged, but only if it's comfortable for you. If you choose to sit in a chair, your feet should be flat on the floor. (You can put a pillow behind your back if you need to sit more forward in the chair.) Assume the same position each time you meditate, so that you automatically associate it with that peaceful, calm state of mind. We recommend that you practice with your eyes closed. Allow yourself to focus on your breathing. Breathing is essential to all that we do, but it also has a natural calming effect, making it easier to reap the benefits of meditation. Don't just hear your breath, feel it. Try not to alter the pattern, but become aware of it. Inhale and exhale through the nostrils, if you can't breathe through your nose, then exhale through your mouth. Take long, deep, slow breaths. Feel the air streaming in as you inhale, and visualize it flowing out of your body as you exhale. As you focus on your breathing, other thoughts will keep popping into your head. That's fine. They will come and then will go. Keep your focus on your breath until the chattering of your mind stops.

Be patient with meditation. After a few weeks you should find that you are calmer and more relaxed. You might be surprised at how energized you feel. As with any exercise, the results are not immediate, but they can be long-term if you keep up the workouts.

And speaking of workouts, meditation can even be used while you're working out, making it an active or moving meditation. You can even do a walking meditation while strolling through a park or on a nature hike during your lunch break. Focus on your movements and your breathing. The more relaxed you are while exercising, the more efficiently you build muscle.

" Grand Master Kim had asked some of the other masters and me to begin an overnight meditation once a month. My coauthor Chris Berlow was a part of the group that attends the overnight meditation, which includes an hour-long hike up Bear Mountain in upstate New York. We sit in a specific area under some pine trees and face east (you are supposed to always face east during meditation because it's good energy). After we hike to the top, we drink wild green tea and then meditate for about two hours. We then take a break, have tea again, and meditate for another one to two hours before we hike back down the mountain.

The very first time we attempted to go on our overnight meditation, there was a tornado and hurricane watch in the lower Hudson Valley area in New York. It was pouring out, but we decided to go anyway because we had told our grand master that we would do it. We packed our supplies and proceeded to hike up the mountain at ten o'clock at night. We got to the top after a great hike, had green tea, and began our meditation. Considering that it was pouring rain, that we had ponchos on, and that it was our first time doing an overnight meditation, it still was one of the best meditations I had ever experienced. The only challenge was when we stopped to take our first break. I hadn't realized that Chris had set up our meditation on an uneven area. Chris was sitting on the elevated side, so all the rain was finding its way to me. When I paused from my meditation, I found I was sitting in a puddle of water. Talk about overcoming adversity and trying to be a good finder. The only good I could find was that it would be a funny story to tell about our meditation experience. "

—PAUL

Meditation plays a key role in your mental development. With time, it becomes easier to analyze and prioritize the events of your day, week, and upcoming year. Meditation acts as a soothing silence and stillness in life, and the benefits are as important as the physical benefits of exercise.

The only way to gain the ability to tap into that higher power, a spiritual power within you that most people don't even know exists, is through relaxation. It is impossible to achieve it if you don't have the ability to relax. We highly recommend that you practice meditation regularly. You may even want to seek out a spiritual leader who teaches meditation techniques. We guarantee, through practice and repetition, you will have the ability to accomplish things you have only dreamed of.

You don't have to be a martial arts master to meditate. At our seminars, we do a focused meditation. We teach students that they need to be comfortable but should not have their back supported, they should align their spine on their own if they can. If they have a medical condition, they should get a back support; otherwise, they should sit in a quiet area in lotus position (one leg on top of the other while the legs are crossed). They should have their back straight, and their left hand placed on their lap, the right hand over it, with the left thumb close to you and the right touching the left. The first step is to have everyone focus on breathing.

Whether you practice a specific form of meditation, learn some easy breathing exercises to let go of that mind chatter, or simply practice a relaxation exercise; these techniques will ease your tension. Utilize your time by practicing breathing while you're driving, on a train, walking or anywhere. However, it's much more effective if you have a designated space that is meant for that purpose, allowing you to escape daily stresses. If you practice the simple meditation techniques in this chapter, you'll be reaping the benefits in no time: A life filled with more calmness and tranquility, with sustainable energy that will last throughout the day.

CHAPTER SUMMARY

- Tapping into a higher power gives you unlimited energy.
- Anyone can meditate, and often we are doing so without consciously realizing it.
- Meditation unlocks the subconscious mind and enables you to tap into a higher power.
- Stress and tension have detrimental impacts on your life; meditation is one of the best methods to eliminate them.
- Breathing is a common cause for many ailments we suffer in life. It helps to maintain a state of calmness and relaxation.
- Most people don't breathe correctly.
- Meditation is the best form of mental exercise.

CHAPTER TEN

Attitude

{
The greatest discovery of any generation
is that a human being can alter his life by
altering his attitude.

—WILLIAM JAMES
}

What is attitude? If you ask ten different people, you'll get ten different answers. Most people have no idea just how powerfully their attitude affects direction and attracts results in their lives. Whatever your goals are—success, health, money, or spirituality—attitude is the fuel for the journey. It is expressed in three ways, through your:

1. Thoughts
2. Feelings
3. Actions

It can't be just one. It's all three. Your thoughts are the foundation for your feelings and actions, and your actions ultimately impact the results. It's the results that we want to improve in our lives.

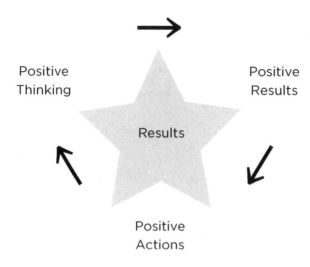

The attitude that you project determines the kind of life you will have.

Your thoughts are revealed to others through your actions. If you project a positive attitude, then positive experiences happen. Unfortunately, it works the same way with a negative attitude. A negative attitude reaps negative results.

Everywhere we turn, there seems to be a predominant focus on negativity. Take local news, for example. Most of the lead stories are based on murders, stabbings, and other criminal activity. Other stories include personal tragedies rather than personal triumphs, reality tv shows based in negativity, or destructive gossip about celebrities and other people's lives rather than their accomplishments. Rarely is there a story focusing on the good of the community. Video games are guilty of the same negative focus. The most successful ones almost always have brutality of some sort in them; some even primarily focus on killing and destructive behavior. Popular music is no different. Music has taken on a predominantly visual aspect. Today it seems that popular songs and videos promoting violence are more popular than ever.

Our youth are exposed to an unlimited stream of media sensation and unsuitable information. With everything available at our fingertips through smartphones it makes it more challenging to monitor what our children are listening to and watching. With all of this negativity impacting our generation, it's a wonder how we get out of bed each morning. It is a sad testament for our culture when people feel better about themselves seeing others in distress. Knocking others down somehow makes people happier. Why? Poor self-esteem? Lack of a positive attitude?

We demonstrate this in our seminars by choosing someone to stand on a table and then asking for three or four volunteers to pull that person down. The volunteers almost never have any trouble doing so. The purpose of this exercise is that the three or four people (poor attitude) symbolize the masses while the one person (positive attitude) on the top symbolizes the leader. We then ask the person standing on the table to pull everyone up on the table. Inevitably people find that pulling others up to their level is much more difficult than trying to pull them down. Pulling people down helps build some people's self esteem and makes them somehow feel superior. This is a dangerous precedent because it encourages people to look for the bad in others as a prerequisite to feeling better. We need to raise our level of awareness as discussed in Chapter 3, to reprogram our minds to have a positive attitude regardless of who and what we are surrounded by. Unfortunately we're often a product of our environments, and sadly this is filled with negativity. One of the major purposes of writing this book is to raise people's awareness about their own attitudes and those around them. Our goal as a company is to create more leaders with positive attitudes who have the ability to stand on the table rather than those standing below.

With all of the negative influences in our culture, it is arduous to keep our attitude positive. It is as if we are fighting an uphill battle because it seems that everywhere we turn there is negativity. The question is, "How do we stay positive and have the strength to not be influenced by our current surroundings?" The answer is simply to train our mind to be a good finder. Every situation that arises in our lives always has a positive side to it. Think back to a traumatic event that affected a large group of people. How did people act? In the wake of Hurricane Katrina, the whole country rallied to help and support the people of New Orleans. This is a testament to the true character and potential within each and every one of us.

Another good example of this is the martial artist we mentioned earlier who injures his right leg. They have trouble walking, and it becomes increasingly difficult to kick with that leg. If that person focuses on the pain and discomfort, then they won't be able to kick effectively, let alone perform other activities. Can we somehow promote a positive attitude with all of these negative thoughts running through our mind? Where is the positive in the above example? The positive is that the martial artist will have a greater appreciation for his or her body and consequently will learn how to train more effectively to prevent the injury. There is also the opportunity to make the other leg more effective while the one is injured. The injury also gives the student a greater understanding of a major martial arts principle known as perseverance and how it applies to any situation. It all comes down to their attitude toward the experience. Positive attitude gives us the ability to get the most out of any experience to live a healthy and vital life. Remember, we all have the ability to choose our thoughts.

At the start of our martial arts classes we always ask our students what is important to a martial artist. They in turn tell us what's important to them and we write it on the board. When a student demonstrates those values they get to write their names on the board as a form of recognition. It is a unique way to inspire students to uphold martial arts values in and out of class. At almost every class a student will say, "Black Belt Attitude." They understand that a black belt is a state of mind, an attitude that we possess, a lifestyle. It is not about earning the black belt or achieving it, it is about applying the values to their everyday life and living the life of a black belt. As quoted in Chris's book, *It's Not About the Belt*, "You don't need to wait for the black belt to encircle your waist. You can live by the code of the Martial Artist, because a black belt encircles your heart."

A man who is master of himself can end a sorrow as easily as he can invent a pleasure. I don't want to be at the mercy of my emotions. I want to use them, to enjoy them, and to dominate them.

—OSCAR WILDE

Are you an emotional puppet?

We all wake up every morning with a choice. We can choose to be negative or positive, lazy or confident, depressed or inspired, sad or happy, mean or nice. We can choose to speak badly about others or to speak well of them. No one controls how you feel except for you. We all have the ability to control how we think, feel, and act. We all have the power to control our mind and emotions. Once we raise our level of awareness and develop this power, life becomes empowering. Is this easy? No. We all endure negative emotions, experiences, and events in our lives. It's okay to think and feel those emotions every now and then, but where people make the mistake is by living there. When something doesn't go their way, they hold on to those negative emotions for the rest of the day, week, month, sometimes even for their entire lives.

Imagine you wake up late one morning for work, get stuck in traffic, and then someone cuts you off. Your morning didn't go as planned and as a result, your whole workday is consumed by negative thought patterns. Your day is ruined. A great analogy for this is touching a burning stove. If you touch the stove while it's hot, your natural reaction is to jerk your hand away. Some people, however, choose to keep their hand on the stove even though it's burning them. These people choose to live in pain.

Have you ever had someone do something you didn't like? For example, you were asked to perform a task you didn't agree with. Or have you ever experienced a time when a situation didn't go as planned, or you got really angry? Of course you have. When you let an event or another person control your emotions, you become an Emotional Puppet. This is when someone allows outside people, situations, circumstances, or events to control how they think, feel, and act. They have no control over the situations in their life, whether good or bad. These Emotional Puppets cannot break out of their state of mind because they have not conditioned themselves to think and feel good. Once we understand the concept, we have the power to control our mind. Again, you have the ability to choose your thoughts. You have infinite power.

Successful people do not allow outside circumstances, situations, events, or people to control how they thnk, feel, and act.

" Conditioning your mind to focus only on the positive and to push away the negatives so they don't control your emotions is not easy. Most people often don't know they are capable of doing so until something dramatic happens. In 1996, my best friend was killed in a motorcycle accident. The day after his accident, I had to teach a martial arts class to twenty-five four- and five-year-olds. I didn't eat or sleep after I found out about the accident. As I sat in my office crying, I wasn't sure what to do. I didn't have anyone to cover my class and couldn't afford to cancel. I had no other choice but to step out on that floor and do what was expected of me: to teach, inspire, motivate, and care for my students. I still was distraught over the death of my friend, but I made a conscious choice to push those feelings aside and be in control of my emotions for the benefit of my students and me. At the time I did not consciously know how the mind worked, but subconsciously I had the ability to be in control. Someone once told me that a pro is a pro regardless. After that day, I realized that I raised my level of awareness and was able to consciously choose to have a positive attitude. **"**

–PAUL

Emotional Puppets have no control over their feelings or actions. They are more likely to react to a negative situation in a negative way and just make things worse. Life is unpredictable. You never know what circumstances it may bring, but never allow someone or something to pull your strings. You don't have to be a victim of circumstance unless you choose to be. It doesn't matter where you've been: what matters is where you're going. Your attitude is much more important than your current appearance, talents, or abilities. No matter how bad your past experiences or present circumstances may be, you should always focus on having a positive attitude regardless of the situation.

Don't focus on the pain of past relationships; focus on the joy and excitement of future ones to be had.

> We awaken in others the same attitude of mind we hold toward them.
>
> —ELBERT HUBBARD

Focus

A positive attitude requires FOCUS

Finding Optimism Consistently Under any Situation

66 In October 1998, I was let go from the Taekwondo School I had been teaching at for more than twelve years. At the time, I had two children, a mortgage, a car payment, and was now unemployed. I had such a sour taste in my mouth, I decided to leave the field of martial arts and pursue a teaching job. After encouragement from Paul and other very close friends, I decided to open Berlow's Taekwondo Academy. Over the first few months of opening my martial arts academy, my wife and I struggled financially. We barely made ends meet and were scrounging to find money to pay the bills. I borrowed $10,000 at 25 percent interest to open the doors to my school. I had a tremendous amount of purpose to make things work. I remember the owner from one of the companies I hired telling me he would probably be taking down the sign in front of the building because most businesses fail in the first year. I told him that I wasn't 'most businesses.' My goal was to get one hundred students by our one-year anniversary, and had two hundred before the end of the year. Now my business flourishes, and I haven't looked back. I couldn't have done this without a positive attitude. 99

—CHRIS

Find the positive in every situation because there almost always is one. In Chapter 7, we described finding the good in every opportunity. Now we want to add positive attitude into that equation. We ask our seminar clients to come up with a challenge and lead them towards finding the opportunity in that challenge. It is our responsibility to find the silver lining in every situation. By finding the good in situations and in others, more good will come to you. Remember, a bad day turns worse unless you gain the ability to shift your mindset. The bad day continues the downward spiral because you are attracting it. Use the same concept to attract the good in life instead. Positive attracts positive and negative attracts negative. Therefore, we must find the good in all events and situations to attract like energy to us. Be a good finder and you will live a happier and more fulfilled life. Stay away and shield yourself from the negative.

66 A few years ago I was having one of the worst mornings of my career. Two clients cancelled their policies, which cost me a significant amount of money. I walked into my office in a very negative frame of mind. Paul and Rick happened to be there, and sensed my negative attitude right away. After explaining to them what had happened, they looked at me with smiles on their faces and said, 'Who's being an emotional puppet now?' They continued to give me a reality check by telling me that I have a choice between allowing others to control my thoughts, turning a bad morning into a terrible day, or choosing to be positive by finding the opportunity in my situation. A light clicked on and I knew that they were right. I was being an emotional puppet, and I am better than that. I immediately changed my attitude to one of positive thoughts. The result was that I had an incredible afternoon, and more than made up for the money that I had lost. 99

—NICK

You Control How You Feel and You Always Choose to Feel Positive.

We've just discussed the importance of being a good finder and how hard it is with the age of technology. Negativity sells, and because this influences what a good majority of people see hear, touch, smell, and taste, this in turn affects how they live their life. Everyone has an excuse for not getting the results they want. They blame their story. People are more apt to point the finger of blame rather than to look internally at themselves. Such people think society owes them something but don't even know what it is. The glass is forever half empty, and other people's hardships make them feel better. Complaining is easier than taking action to correct their problems.

We all know or have seen people just like we've described above. They live in their own world and feel they have the right to act any way they choose. However, we can't let their attitude affect our way of thinking. We have to be strong enough in who we are to withstand their negative tendencies and to not let them bring us down.

Now that we've gotten all the negativity out of the way, we can finally focus on the good stuff. Let's get back to who we are and what we're about—the positive side of life. The people who look at the glass as half full always find the good in every situation. They are good finders. Situations are challenges not obstacles. A challenge excites us, while an obstacle weighs us down. Positive people live a very purposeful life and view each day as a new opportunity. They take advantage of these new opportunities by putting their energy into whatever is in front of them. They focus on their Worthy Ideal and Life's Purpose. They believe that they could make a difference simply by having the right attitude. You will always see them smiling and going out of their way to make someone else happy. They spend their energy finding solutions rather than complaining. These are action-oriented people who love to live and enjoy life to the fullest. They are masters of their lives and wake up each morning choosing to be positive. No one influences how they feel because they are in the driver's seat and are always focused on what's ahead. These are people you are naturally drawn to and love to be around.

66 One evening after dinner, I decided to take my children to Carvel, a local ice cream franchise. Our usual location was closed, so we drove another fifteen minutes to another. The owner was an elderly, immigrant man, who had the most positive attitude I have ever seen. He was so grateful for our business and treated my children with genuine kindness and friendliness. He had a smile so wide and loved kids. Once he served us, I purposely asked my kids to watch how he was with the other customers. The smile never left his face, and he clearly took pleasure in serving others and had pride in his business. I then gave what my kids would call one of my many 'fatherly lectures,' pointing out to them that here is a gentleman who no doubt worked twelve-hour days and made very little money yet was obviously happy with his life and had an engaging, infectious personality. On the car ride home, I told my kids that no matter where life leads them, if they have only one choice in life, then they should always choose to have a positive attitude. From then on, we've tried to make it a point to drive those extra fifteen minutes for ice cream, specifically because of this man's positive attitude. 99

—RICK

So how do we avoid the negative and gravitate to the positive? We must gain the ability and awareness to separate the two. As you go through your day, look closely at how people present themselves. Do they have positive body language and smile often or do they slump their shoulders and have a constant frown?

FILL OUT THE ATTITUDE EVALUATION BELOW TO FIND OUT IF THOSE AROUND YOU ARE AFFECTING YOUR ATTITUDE.

LIST TEN PEOPLE YOU SPEND THE MOST TIME WITH.	HOW DOES IT AFFECT YOUR ATTITUDE?
1.	
2.	
3.	
4.	
5.	
6.	
7.	
8.	
9.	
10.	

Take time and think about the individuals in your life that you list as negative and those you list as positive. Think about your family, friends, and coworkers. Who looks at the glass as half full, and who looks at it as half empty? Who is always happy and who is always complaining? As you put your list together, you will get a better understanding of who you are and who you surround yourself with.

Your friends are a reflection of your attitude toward life. You are born into your family and your friends are acquired over time. You'll always have an association with your family, so set an example for those who are negative. An important point to mention is that no matter how much you attempt to help them, they have to be willing to improve. In some cases, you just have to accept and love them no matter what their attitude is like. Think of the old saying, "You can lead a horse to water but you can't make it drink."

> The best way to inspire people to superior performance is to convince them by everything that you do and by your everyday attitude that you are whole-heartedly supporting them.
>
> —HAROLD S. GENEEN

Surrounding Yourself with Like-Minded People.

We all have a certain amount of mental energy. Eventually you will become drained if you continually attempt to lift negative people up but get no results. Avoid negative behavior. If you encourage their negative attitude by agreeing with them, when in your heart you disagree, or if you give them constant sympathy, they will never improve. You may make them feel better in the short-term, but in the long-term they are doomed to repeat the behavior. Remember time bandits and how they zap the energy right out of you; you may find that a friendship is more work than it's worth. This is when you have to make the decision to move on and not let them bring you down.

Be a positive person and surround yourself with positive people; soon you will be acting with black belt character. A black belt always looks for the positive

The Attitude of Gratitude

An attitude of gratitude is based on your perception. Gratitude is the natural feeling that comes when you recognize the real value of the people and things in your life. Focus on the good, and you cannot help but have a better attitude and experience of life. Gratitude, then, is something you can encourage, something you can learn.

Your life is better when you feel blessed, when you can look around and say, "Thank you." When you see life as a wonderful gift, your experience is a richer one. Gratitude is possibly the most powerful way to improve your life. The power of gratitude is this: the more that you are grateful for, the more positive experiences you will have. So how do you begin to create an attitude of gratitude? One of the greatest ways we have found to develop the habit of expressing gratitude is write a Gratitude Journal. When you write down what you are grateful for, it puts your life in an entirely new perspective. You realize how much abundance you already have, right at that very moment. Keeping a Gratitude Journal allows you to stay focused on all that is good in your life. Subconsciously you begin to expect more good things to come your way. It teaches you and gets you in the habit of becoming a good finder.

You don't already have a Gratitude Journal? No problem, we'll help you get started. In the space below, foster your own attitude of gratitude by writing.

LIST TWENTY ITEMS YOU'RE GRATEFUL FOR IN YOUR LIFE:

1.

2.

3.

4.

5.

6.

7.

8.

9.

10.

11.

12.

13.

14.

15.

16.

17.

18.

19

20.

Now that we've helped you get started, it's time for you to do the rest. Go out and get your own Gratitude Journal to write your thoughts in. Your journal is very personal and should reflect who you truly are. Let your thoughts flow and write whatever first comes to mind.

66 My wife always kept several journals and often I would see her writing in them. In my subconscious, I wondered what and why she was writing. Coincidentally, in one of our Empowered Mastery meetings Paul mentioned that he and his wife kept a Gratitude Journal. When I told him about my wife's journals he suggested that my wife and I should start one together. My old self would have immediately laughed this off with some sarcastic remark, but this is the new me, the one that has learned and still is learning to have a positive attitude and to think with an open mind. That night I suggested to my wife that we keep a Gratitude Journal and she immediately smiled and said that would be a great idea. The next night while my wife and I were in bed she gave me a colorful notebook with a picture of both of us on the cover. She said this would be our new Gratitude Journal. We then took turns writing down three things that went well during the day. It wasn't easy at the start, especially with four kids and both of us working. However, we made sure to write every night and even made a game out of it by seeing if we came up with the same things. As the days and weeks went on, I found that I was training my mind to be a good finder. I learned to find the good in any situation, no matter how stressful my day was. 99

—RICK

An attitude of gratitude is a powerful way to change your life. When you focus on all there is to be grateful for, then you will notice there are more things to be grateful for, and as you notice more things to be grateful for, the list will become endless.

CHAPTER SUMMARY

- Your attitude reflects the results you get in life.
- Positive attracts positive.
- Your attitude is a combination of your thoughts, feelings, and actions.
- Be in control over your emotions. Don't be an Emotional Puppet.
- Become a good finder.
- Surround yourself with those who share your outlook on life.
- Be grateful.

CHAPTER ELEVEN

Track Your Goals

{
A goal without a plan is just a wish.
—**LARRY ELDER**
}

I know what some of you might be thinking: not another book about goal setting. If you're in the business arena, no doubt you've taken classes or enrolled in some sort of seminar on goal setting. We do agree that goal setting can be paramount to achieving success in your professional and personal life. But rather than reiterate what everyone says, we would like to tackle it from an uncommon perspective.

During our seminars and programs we love to ask the following question to business professionals, 'How many of you have ever set a goal?' Inevitably, everyone in the room will raise their hand. Then we ask, 'How many of you have achieved every goal that you set?' Most of the hands in the room go down. For the 'million dollar' question, we then ask, 'Why?'

We get answers like:
- It was too difficult or unrealistic.
- It took too long.
- I lost interest.
- I got sidetracked.
- It wasn't important.

Although all of these answers can be true, the real answer to our question is that most goals that are not achieved do not align with our Worthy Ideal.

GOALS AND YOUR WORTHY IDEAL

In the Awareness and Realization chapters, we spoke about the importance of creating and living through your Worthy Ideal. We also mentioned that all uncommonly successful people throughout history had a Worthy Ideal that drove them. If we look at Martin Luther King as an example, we already know that his Worthy Ideal was civil rights and equality for all. This is what drove and consumed him.

All the rallies and speeches he made, including the march on Washington in 1963, were goals. Furthermore, he had a burning desire to achieve all of his goals, because they were aligned with his Worthy Ideal. If Dr. King had set a goal of making a million dollars, do you think he would have achieved it? Do you think he would have been passionate about it? Of course not, because it was not aligned with his Worthy Ideal. It had nothing to do with his true purpose and passion in life, civil rights.

All successful people have a true burning desire to live through their Worthy Ideal. If the goals you set are not aligned with your Worthy Ideal, there is a true disconnect. We often see our clients set goals that are not really theirs: they have someone else telling them what they should be achieving.

A good majority of our clients are salespeople. They are often told by their managers to come in to work on Monday and make 50 calls so they can make 10 appointments to make 3 sales. How inspired can you truly be in an attempt to achieve goals that weren't yours in the first place?

Nick has a better idea, one that he teaches all of our business clients: how about making 5 calls, 5 appointments, and inspiring 5 people to take action to improve their financial lives. Which one sounds better?

What makes martial arts so successful in the very goal oriented western world is the belt system. Traditionally, all students start as a white belt representing innocence. As the white belt gets more soiled through training it gets darker ultimately become black. That is why a black belt is the highest rank in our training. When the black belt becomes frayed through over use and consistent training, it becomes white again, returning to innocence. Over the years, the belt system has been modified where students train to advance to a higher rank. The higher the rank, the darker the belt color. This helps martial artists set short-term goals such as individual belt ranks to achieve longer-term goals by obtaining different levels of black belt. It is through the tracking and accomplishment of achieving the new ranks that students gain the confidence to achieve unparalleled success.

{ Set your goals high, and don't stop till you get there.

—BO JACKSON }

{ "You are never too old to set another goal or to dream a new dream."

—C. S. LEWIS }

Prioritize Your Goals

Don't get us wrong: goals are important. They inspire us and motivate us. Once you've developed a goal or a set of goals that you can realistically achieve, you need to decide how relatively important these goals are to you, as you can only focus effectively on a few goals at a time. Also, it is often helpful to have an overall goal that is most important to you, as this provides a sense of direction and focus. Then, with this primary orientation, you can concentrate your energy on achieving your purpose.

Using the space below, write down all of your goals as quickly as you can. Don't think about them or judge them, just write them. Some goals may be very general, some very specific, some long-term, and some short-term. It doesn't matter; just write down whatever comes to you. You may write some of the same goals from previous exercises, or you may find other goals surfacing as well. Keep going until you feel yourself slowing down and then concentrate for perhaps another minute or so until you feel you've exhausted all ideas.

Goals

1.

2.

3.

4.

5.

6.

7.

8.

9.

10.

11.

12.

13.

14.

15.

16.

17.

18.

19.

20.

Now review your goals and ask yourself this very important question: are they aligned with your Worthy Ideal?

My Goals

When setting and tracking your goals, you should ask yourself why you want to achieve them. Let's take the common goal of losing weight. Most people approach this task by asking themselves what they have to do in order to lose the weight. That is thinking from the outside in, and is why diets are a billion dollar industry. People go on and then off of diets over and over again. We're sure you know someone like that, and it might even be you. The real question you should ask yourself is why you want to lose the weight.

People think it's the goal that's going to get them excited, but it's actually the purpose behind the goal that is most important. Take the example of making a million dollars. It's not the money per se but the feeling of exhilaration that you experience by achieving the goal that is exciting. Understanding this is important because if you attach a feeling or emotion to the right part of a goal, then it will make it more realistic to you. You want to feel this sense of accomplishment all the time. Again, it's not necessarily the goal that inspires us but what you will get from it. Just saying, "I want to make a million dollars," might not be enough to inspire you to achieve it, but when you attach the feeling of accomplishment along with it, you will give yourself the confidence that "I can do anything." You may think that a million dollars is what you really want but it's the feeling that you are going to receive from accomplishing the goal that gets you pumped. It's all the stuff you can do with it that truly motivates you, and the positive feeling you get from attaining that goal that is most important. In the space below, write your goals again but this time in the column next to it write down your purpose for this goal as well.

Goal	Purpose
1.	
2.	
3.	
4.	
5.	
6.	

7.

8.

9.

10.

11.

12.

13.

14.

15.

16.

17.

18.

19.

20.

21.

22.

23.

24.

25.

26.

27.

28.

Now in the space below, prioritize your goals, with 1 as the most important and 20 as the least.

Their Importance

1.

2.

3.

4.

5.

6.

7.

8.

9.

10.

11.

12.

13.

14.

15.

16.

17.

18.

19.

20.

Finally, assign a time line for when you wish to accomplish these goals, whether in weeks, months, or years. The purpose of these exercises is first and foremost to get you to think about your goals and their importance and purpose. This helps to clear your mind and provides you with the tools needed to focus on, one goal at one time. Once you've accomplished one, then you can move on to the next and the next, and before long (like most successful people), you'll be able to accomplish more than one goal at the same time.

> If you can find a path with no obstacles, it probably doesn't lead anywhere.
>
> —FRANK A. CLARK

Common Obstacles to Goals

Obstacles can be anything or anyone getting in the way of you reaching your goals. Realizing that there are going to be obstacles along the way to achieving your goal makes it easier to plan for, overcome, and avoid them. Before you can remove an obstacle, you first need to recognize it. You are responsible for overcoming your challenges and creating new opportunities; no one else is. The moment you are able to learn and accept this, your life will become more fulfilling. Once you take responsibility for your actions, you will be able to think of ways to maneuver around those obstacles standing between you and your goals.

Identifying potential obstacles can help you develop a plan to deal with them. Here are the ten most common obstacles:

1. Poor attitude
2. F.A.D. (fear, anxiety, and doubt)
3. Lack of confidence
4. Poor self-image
5. No vision
6. Not aligned with your worthy ideal.
7. Procrastination

8. Lack of ambition
9. Poor time management
10. Negative influences

Many people have no clear idea or vision about what they want in life while others want too much. In both cases, they will never achieve anything because they lack focus. People often set up unrealistic, impossible goals for themselves. Perhaps they are being too vague about what they want. Saying, "I'd like to be rich" is too general; there are no specifics to focus on. On the other hand, a goal shouldn't be short-term or very easy to achieve, like "I'm going to make one extra sales call today" or "I'll stick to my exercise regimen for a week." Yet another obstacle occurs when people don't feel an intense conviction or burning desire that they really want something, like better health or more money. Some people don't prioritize what they want and are unable to determine how important achieving a goal is to them. So they diffuse their energy by going after the less important items instead of concentrating on what they truly desire. To set and achieve your goals, you must:

1. Have a clear and specific image of what you want.
2. Determine if your goals are realistic.
3. Act with conviction in the pursuit of your goal.

These questions are designed to help you better know yourself, so that you can make the appropriate decisions about setting your goals.

Commit to Your Goals

Besides setting a clear goal, you also need to create a goal you can realistically achieve, and then be truly committed to it. Don't let your goals fall by the wayside because you failed to plan for them. Goal setting and goal achievement are much easier if you COMMIT to a series of steps to achieve them.

Choose. You need to make a conscious decision. This is the first step to any goal. How much do you want or desire your goal. Weak desires bring weak results, just as a strong sense of want and willingness to do whatever it takes brings accomplishment. You've got to really, really want to achieve the goal.

Outlook. What is your attitude toward this goal? Positive? Negative? We learned in Chapter 10 how important attitude is. Can you actually see yourself achieving this goal? What will your achievement feel like? How will your life unfold differently as a result? If the goal is something tangible, then we recommend that you carry a goal card with you (more about this later in this chapter) so that you are reminded of it every day. If you can't picture yourself achieving the goal, chances are you won't.

Make a plan. Create action steps to follow for accomplishing this goal. Identify key achievements along the way—the most important steps that must happen for the goal to become a reality. A builder can't start a construction project without a blueprint. In the same way, you can't construct your goals without a clear plan of what you want.

Map out your way. Commit to achieving your goal by writing it down. Write down the plan, the action steps, and then map out the best route for accomplishment. Writing down the goal, the plan, and a timeline sets events in motion that may not have happened otherwise.

Invest time every day toward your goal. Establish specific times for checking your progress. This enables you to take an inventory of your actions. This practice helps you to see if there are any areas that need improvement or change. Life changes on a daily basis, and this can cause interference with your goals. Take a look at all of the factors in your life that keep you from accomplishing your goals and then develop a plan to overcome them.

Track your overall progress regularly. You must move forward. If you aren't advancing, analyze why that goal is not being met. Don't allow the goal to just fade away. Figure out what you need to do to accomplish it.

" When I first opened my martial arts school, I had to take out a $10,000 loan at 25 percent interest. I also joined a martial arts organization to help with billing and tuition collections. The organization had a Top Ten Award for individuals who grossed the top ten tuition collections. In the first year, my wife and I went to their convention and received an award for most promising new school. I had to come up and give an acceptance speech. I told the audience that when I returned next year, I would be a top ten school. A year went by and a month before the convention, I knew it was going to be close and called every day to see what my collections were. They wouldn't tell me and said they would have the announcement at the annual banquet. It turned out I didn't just make the top ten; I was the number four school in the organization. Here I was, with my wife and me up in front of the banquet, very excited about our accomplishment. During my acceptance speech, I pushed the envelope further by saying next year I would be driving down in a new, yellow Hummer (the original kind). The following year, we had continued success and the school was flourishing. At the next convention I said during my acceptance speech, 'Last year I declared that my wife and I would drive down in a brand new yellow Hummer. I'm sorry to say I didn't because I decided to buy a black one instead.' But it wasn't purchasing the Hummer that was really great. It was the fact that I had set out a high goal and did whatever it took to achieve that goal. A very close friend of mine, who drove down from New York to Florida in the Hummer (I would never do that again), said that I had done more for the martial arts industry than I will ever know because I gave many others the belief that they can do it. I will admit that although it was a wonderful goal and I am happy and grateful that I achieved it, my house in Vermont was a cheaper monthly payment then my Hummer. "

—CHRIS

Going for the "Goal"

We've talked about the importance of goal setting. Goals give you a purpose, a direction in life. But the whole point of setting goals in the first place is to achieve them, right? Each of us learns in a different way, so no one technique works for everyone. People usually have a predominate style of learning—kinesthetic, auditory, or visual, so why not apply this to achieving goals?

Kinesthetic. Writing down your goals is crucial. When you commit an action to paper, you're also committing to it in your subconscious mind. Furthermore, consistently writing down your goals reinforces the concept of repetition, which is a key ingredient to embedding any desire in your subconscious mind. (Please refer back to Chapter 1 where we talk about the subconscious mind.)

Auditory. Create audio recordings in your own voice for each goal. Play these recordings back at least twice a day to reinforce them. We suggest you do this when you get out of bed in the morning and again before you go to sleep. Use music to help reinforce them. Here's a suggestion: while driving, instead of listening to the same station playing the same songs or preaching the same message, listen to audio books that motivate or inspire you. It can be an extremely productive use of time

Visual. Create a vision board of what you want. Cut out pictures from magazines or print images from the Internet to reinforce the vision of what you desire. Change your screensaver to pictures or statements of your goals. Using pop-up reminders can also be a great way to reinforce your dreams.

Goal Cards

Earlier we mentioned Goals Cards. For many of us, identifying goals is difficult, and we often lack the focus to accomplish our goals. A Goal Card provides a structured process for identifying specific goals of your own choosing. The Goal Card helps to:

- Identify and prioritize goals
- Set specific goals to work toward
- Put our goals in our subconscious minds through repetition (but only if you read your goal card every day).

The act of identifying needs and setting goals is motivating in itself. When people set their own goals, then they are more likely to follow through and maintain progress once the goal is reached. Just having a Goal Card is extremely empowering. It says, in effect, "This is your life. You are in charge of deciding how to live it. You are capable of making good choices."

With these cards, individuals identify and prioritize action steps that are necessary to change their lives for the better. They set specific and meaningful goals. The process allows for setting small goals, many of which will be readily achievable, which leads to more success, enhances confidence, and increases motivation for further change.

We feel so strongly about committing to our goals to paper that we use our business cards as our Goal cards.

Goal Card Rules

Here are some helpful hints for writing your Goal Cards:

Each has to begin with, "I am so happy and grateful now that…"

Each has to be a specific and realistic goal. For example, if you just say "I want to lose weight," that's not enough. You have to say, "I want to lose twenty pounds."

Each must determine exactly what you intend to do or give in return for your goal. (There is no such thing as something for nothing.) For example, if my goal is to make a million dollars, then I will give back by teaching seminars, writing a book, and helping other people live a better life.

Each has to have a target date.

Each must be written as a statement.

Sample Goal Card

I am so happy and grateful now that I have lost twenty pounds.

I am so happy and grateful that I have lost twenty pounds by waking up an hour earlier every morning to run.

I am so happy and grateful that in six months from today, (write a specific date) ...

EXAMPLES OF PAST GOAL CARDS

RICK'S GOAL CARD

Target date January 1, 2009

I am so happy and grateful now that I have made the decision to live a healthier life.

My goal is to improve my eating habits – I want to eat a fruit and vegetable every single day for six months

My goal is to begin an exercise program – I want to work out every single day for a year.

PAUL'S GOAL CARD

Target date January 31, 2009

I am so happy and grateful now that I am living a healthy, vital, and energetic life with my family. I am so grateful and appreciative now that I am a multimillionaire, operating profitable businesses, financially free and abundant. I am excited now that I am coaching and teaching millions of people across the world to achieve their personal full potential in all areas of their lives.

NICK'S GOAL CARD

Target date December 31, 2009

I am so happy and grateful now that I am living a happy, healthy, vibrant, and abundant lifestyle. I will earn three million dollars and have a body fat level of 12 percent by the end of 2009. This will allow me the freedom to provide a lifestyle for my family that my wife and I have always dreamed about.

CHRIS' GOAL CARD

Target date September 1, 2010

I am so happy and grateful that I have a loving relationship with my son Brandon. He is successful in all his endeavors and we treat each other with love and respect.

I am so happy and grateful that I am in my new martial arts facility with 600 students, with my dream team supporting me all the way.

Goal setting is fundamental to achieving success in any endeavor. Every great accomplishment in any area of life can be attributed to having a very clear and specific goal. The challenge is that we've heard about goal setting so often that we tend to ignore the process because we think we know it all. However, unless you practice these concepts on a regular basis, then you will find yourself falling back into bad habits.

With setting goals we create our destiny and live through our Worthy Ideal. We all have goals whether we are consciously aware of them or not. The difficulty is that most of us aren't inspired enough to accomplish them. People often become frustrated and give up on their goals too early, which results in the feeling of un-fulfillment. We need goals that inspire us. Compelling goals have the power to move us to transform our lives. Goal setting and goal achieving both force you to challenge yourself to reach new heights you never thought possible. Remember, you must make sure that your goals are in alignment with your Worthy Ideal that we spoke about in Chapter 3.

Without goals, we have no clear direction of where we want to go in life. Living life without goals is like getting into a car and not knowing where you are going. If we jump into a vehicle and begin to drive, we eventually end up saying, "Where are we going and why are we going there?" We should always be consciously aware of what our goals are and what their purpose is, what the plan of action is to obtain them, and what the target date for accomplishing them is. Think of the goal setting process as a built-in navigation system. You enter your goal, and it shows how to get there, where and when to turn, and what the exact arrival time will be.

We need to set goals for how we are going to live our lives in every area—emotionally, spiritually, physically, financially, and in our relationships and our attitudes. Set goals for the kind of person you are committed to become. Something happens as soon as you set goals. Almost instantaneously, you change, because the expectation for yourself and for your life changes.

You acknowledge to both your conscious and subconscious minds that you are not satisfied with where you are and that you are always seeking ways to improve.

Pursuing our dreams in life is important because they have the power to propel us forward. But more importantly, keep in mind that we need to realize that when our lives come to an end it will not be how much money we have, what type of car we drive, or how big our house is that will matter; it will be who we became as persons. When we remember someone close to us who has passed on, we do not focus on the possessions they left behind but instead focus on whom the person was. Your life has meaning once your goals fall in alignment with your Worthy Ideal and Life's Purpose. As with any recipe, you must have all of the ingredients to get the best results. Each ingredient is necessary for the final result. Below is Empowered Mastery's Life Alignment Blueprint.

WORTHY IDEAL

LIFE PURPOSE

AREAS OF LIFE

GOALS

As you see, all of the above are key ingredients to living the life you choose.

Goals direct our focus. It is important to have goals to help direct our thoughts and minds to focus on what we desire most in our lives. Set your goals, regardless of previous "failures." Remember, most successful people have failed at one time or another. Start anew and do it properly. Come from a place of faith and belief and then watch your life soar to greater heights of happiness and fulfillment. Above all, enjoy life, for it is a gift. Live it with passion. Everything you need is there. Just go get it. It's yours for the taking.

Reward Yourself

One last point about goals: We work so hard to achieve them that we fail to reward ourselves. Instead we tend to say, 'ok, what's next?' When setting goals, think about a reward when you achieve it. It doesn't have to be grandiose like a vacation or a new car, it could be something small like going to your favorite restaurant or movie. Whatever it is, take the time to celebrate your accomplishment. You deserve it!

CHAPTER SUMMARY

- Start setting goals one at a time.
- Prioritize your goals.
- COMMIT.
- Make sure your goals are aligned with your Worthy Ideal.
- Reward yourself.

[CHAPTER TWELVE]

Imagination

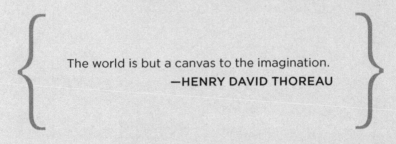

The world is but a canvas to the imagination.
—HENRY DAVID THOREAU

Imagination is what separates us from every other living creature on this planet. Our life and everything around us is a product of our imagination. Expand your horizon and you'll find the world itself expands. As you access the power of your imagination, inspiration will flow to and throughout you. As you fill your subconscious with thoughts of what you would like to experience, you bring anything you desire into your life. Imagination is the language through which you communicate with the universe. As you develop your body through physical exercise, so also can you develop your imagination through Mind Muscle Exercises.

Your imagination creates the future. Challenge yourself to make your life match your vision. No matter the current circumstance, imagination gives us the ability to transform any situation that does not match our perceived destiny and to free us from our past. Your past experiences no longer hold you captive. Most people never engage their imagination because they don't believe anything better exists or don't have the confidence to follow through with their dreams.

Everything we need to succeed in life has already been created.

Our imagination expands what already exists in the realm of the universe. Look at everything around us and all of the new technology at our fingertips. Everything changes at an incredible rate. The computer you buy today is obsolete tomorrow. This is all due to our imagination and our ability to create. Imagination is the offspring of our thoughts. If our minds are always picking up on different vibrations and are open to new ideas, then it's important to capture these diverse thoughts on paper so we can utilize them later in life.

Imagination is the creative mind constantly thinking and rejuvenating old ideas into new concepts. Look at the example below:

Supercomputer Processors ⟶ Home PC ⟶ Laptop ⟶ iPhone

This illustrates revamping an old concept into a new one. The primary function of the creative part of your mind is to organize your imagination and manifest these new thoughts in reality. If you combine the power of this with the action of the creative part of your brain, then you will be able to implement anything you want in life. This will ultimately set you apart from the rest of society. Think about it, most people still cling to old methods and status quo results.

The way to fulfill your destiny is to use this creative force to develop the life of your dreams. In the previous chapter, we focused on tracking your goals. Imagination is an integral part of the goal setting process and is both interpretative and creative. This means that it can receive impressions and ideas and can also use these impressions and ideas to form new combinations of the same. So, any one of us can take information from endless sources and transform it into endless new combinations. Having an infinite number of new combinations or ideas is, without debate, one of the most valuable tools we can possess in our life. The city of Dubai provides a remarkable example of this. In 1991, Dubai was nothing more than a few buildings among the sand. Today, through imagination, the once barren city hosts some of the world's most innovative structures:

1. Palm Island. An additional eighty miles of coast was created in the form of three artificial islands in the shape of a palm tree. These islands are home to apartments, hotels, and shopping.
2. The World. Approximately three hundred artificial islands are arranged in the shape of the world.
3. Burj Dubai. This half-mile high tower is the tallest in the world.
4. Hydropolis. The hotel is completely submerged under water with each room having a panoramic view of the ocean.
5. Dubailand Ski Dome. An indoor ski resort in the middle of the desert with six thousand tons of real snow.

Imagination reveals discoveries once thought impossible. It all begins with a fantasy. Creativity fuels the inner workings of your mind, along with hope, and faith. For every challenge there is a solution. Throughout the world, people are using their imagination at an ever-increasing rate to constantly create and achieve what was previously thought impossible. If your mind can dream it and believe it, then you can achieve it. It reminds us that we have control and mastery over our own destinies. The question is can you dream? Can you believe? Of course you can.

Imagination is often thought of as a fantasy. This might be partly true, but to say that that is all it is severely underestimates the full power of the faculty. Your personality, self-image, and the way you see life are determined by your imagination. Imagination is an asset or liability depending on how you use it. You can imagine you can't do anything right or always look at the worst-case scenario. The glass is always half empty. On the other hand, you can use imagination productively to lead to greater success. Many people get stuck on auto-pilot because they're not using their intellectual qualities. Successful people make effective use of their imagination on a daily basis. They have a mental picture of what they want to accomplish and make adjustments as they learn from their mistakes. The unsuccessful keep doing the same thing but expect different results. Have you ever heard the phrase, "The definition of insanity is doing the same thing over and over again expecting another result?" Personal growth is an ongoing process. You should constantly evaluate your life. Actions that aren't producing the results you desire should be replaced with actions that do. Open your mind and use your imagination to better yourself. We all have negative voices in our head. Do not let these thoughts become prevalent. Learn to develop positive thoughts and attitudes to counteract negative ones that enter your mind.

Picture yourself at the top of your field. Imagine what it would be like. Think of the goals you listed. Push negative thoughts away and plan for a better future for you and your family. Act like you are successful now. Use your "I AM" statements. Develop more confidence by celebrating your past successes. Most people fail to advance in life because they do not believe they can do better. Tell yourself you can. Start believing and you will. Master Yoda from the groundbreaking movie Empire Strikes Back says it best, "Do or do not. There is no try."

Worthy Ideals arise from our use of our imagination, which leads to a world of unbelievable sights, sounds, and sensations. It empowers us to make sense of descriptions that are remote to our times or foreign to our experience. Using his untapped creativity, Mozart heard silent music, and the Wright brothers created a vehicle that could fly through the skies. Einstein considered imagination even more important than knowledge.

Our imagination uses what we do know and reconfigures images into something unique.

> Imagination will often carry us to worlds that never were. But without it we go nowhere.
>
> —CARL SAGAN

What is 'That Box?'

One of the biggest catch phrases today is "think outside the box." If you can't think outside the box, then you aren't using your full creative potential. For us, before we could truly think outside the box, we had to figure out what the box was. Basically, the box this refers to is your current thought process. It encompasses any assumptions you make. Thinking outside the box requires drawing on your intellectual qualities and going beyond your five senses.

Below is a Conditioning Exercise to test your imagination. In the space provided, there are nine dots. Connect all nine dots with four lines without taking your pen or pencil off the paper.

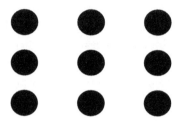

Now that we've solved the mystery of the box, let's imagine for a moment that our lives are confined in that box like the picture above. The only contact with the outside world we have is through pictures, through our five senses, and what others have told us. Even the best pictures and the most accurate descriptions can't describe the outside surroundings. As a result, you may have all sorts of assumptions that are not accurate.

The box is a great metaphor for our limited thinking. Our thoughts and assumptions are like those pictures and descriptions that form the sides of your box, limiting what you can see or know about the world. So what can you do? Simple—climb over the side and break through.

> Imagination is the living power and prime agent of all human perception.
>
> —SAMUEL TAYLOR COLERIDGE

We have taken thousands of children and adults from a state of non-believers to confident black belts in our professional martial arts careers. It always starts by helping the novice students paint a picture in their heads and imagine themselves achieving their black belts. In doing this, students take on the identity of black belts far before they actually achieve it. This is because they have already accomplished it in their minds.

Unleashing Your Imagination and Creativity

The limitations we place upon ourselves are just as unreal as what is happening in a movie, because we have chosen to hold on to something fictitious. However, while we must accept the reality of the moment, we are not bound in it forever. We can change the future with our imaginations. The personal limitations you have accepted can be relinquished anytime you wish. Through persistent imagination, you can discard an old script and start a completely new story. You can free yourself from the paralyzing paradigms and misconceptions that are holding you back and have all that you truly desire. All you need to do is to have faith and believe in the unknowing. The following Conditioning Exercise stimulates your imagination.

Previously, we asked you to be the Picasso of your life, but your awareness then may not have been what it is now. Use your imagination to attract the true life you desire. Remember—you have infinite power. Pretend you are the director and writer of your personal movie. Anything is possible in it. With that in mind, now create what we call your life script statement. Below is Paul's:

I am internally vital, physically strong, emotionally balanced, and spiritually centered. I feel younger and more flexible every single day. My wife and I have a loving, passionate, fun, exciting, honest, and respectful marriage. Our children are healthy, happy, educated, athletic, beautiful, focused, determined, disciplined, organized, confident, respectful, and appreciative people. My brother and I have a successful, profitable, and abundant martial arts business. Our students, their families, and our staffs are happy, dedicated, loyal, appreciative, and passionate. We positively impact thousands of people within our community by teaching martial arts. My partners and I have a successful, profitable, and abundant martial arts franchise and consulting business. Our franchisees and clients are happy, dedicated, loyal, appreciative, passionate, and profitable. They receive tremendous value from utilizing our martial arts business systems. My partners and I have a successful, profitable, and abundant public speaking and personal development business. We help millions of people around the world to rediscover their inner strength and their power of achievement by utilizing the power of their mind. My brother and I have multiple real estate investments and additional streams of income. My family and I are financially free and abundant. We travel around the world as a family. I am a leader for my entire family. I keep my family together.

NOW IN THE SPACE BELOW WRITE YOUR LIFE SCRIPT STATEMENT.

Life Script Statement

You are constantly running a mental movie with you as star. These images determine your personal behavior and the kind of life you lead. You have the power to mentally create a new life for yourself. Whatever you visualize, you can have it. All you must do is imagine yourself as having achieved your desire. We call it the truth in advance.

The most riveting and exciting aspect of imagination is how we can choreograph mental images of what doesn't exist yet in the physical world. Take Walt Disney—he took a simple cartoon mouse and transformed him into the largest entertainment resort in the world. He felt so strongly in the power and strength of imagination that he called his engineers "Imagineers."

We are also able to construct new ideas stimulated by and building upon our previous experiences. Combining imagination with creativity gives us more than just mental images. It causes things to come into existence, it makes or originates, and it produces and brings about. When we creatively imagine something, we actually cause it to come into being because it has been formed, for the first time, in our minds. This allows us to transform our lives through the power of creative imagination.

Whatever idea you hold in your imagination—whether it is negative or positive, constructive or destructive—imagination will bring forth its own kind.

Creative imagination is a powerful force. It can be used to overcome disease, poverty and depression, and push the human body to exceptional feats. No situation is hopeless. Every obstacle has a resolution. Obstacles are really just opportunities in disguise. We need to carefully examine every so-called crisis in our lives for the hidden opportunity in it.

Our conscious mind limits us because it is dependent on the outside world.

Air Force Colonel George Hall is a dramatic example of this. During the Vietnam War, he was locked in a pitch-black cell in a North Vietnamese prison camp for seven years. Instead of focusing on his current environment, he instead spent his days imagining himself playing a full round of golf. One week after he was released from the POW camp, he shot a seventy-six at the Greater New Orleans Open. Such is the power of our imaginations. Since our senses often deceive us, we frequently accept false concepts, values, and beliefs. The conscious mind is objective. It observes and is rational. We gain our willpower though our conscious mind, which often inhibits our creative process.

What we see with our conscious mind often deceives us. When you look at a long string of utility poles or power lines, they usually appear to decrease in size and merge into one line. How many times have you heard the story of the man wandering the desert chasing after an elusive pool of water only to find that it is sand? These distortions are the result of false images and messages from our conscious minds. Faulty images are accepted from our conscious minds, and we choose to perpetuate them in our subconscious minds.

What do you see in the following picture?

Do you see a vase or two faces?

To free ourselves from the limitations of our conscious minds, we must turn inward. To continue to look for inspiration externally is to continue to experience those conditions that have been holding us back. For this reason, we explore our subconscious mind to change any false beliefs into positive and constructive ones. Through repetition and impact you intentionally program them into your sub-conscious mind.

In Chapter 1, we discussed reprogramming your subconscious mind. You are not powerless against it. It does not control you. But, because you are unaware of this, you have lacked the imagination and creativity to improve your life. Throughout the centuries, successful people have either intuitively or knowingly become aware that they too possessed a power over their mind. They called on this power to help them imagine and create great works of art, music, dance, inventions, literature, and empires. This is what we described in this book as our IQ's.

Many untapped talents and unlimited capabilities are hidden deep within your subconscious, but it can't motivate itself. You have to command it to work for your benefit. This will bring about whatever you most persistently impress upon it. It is a valued, competent, and trustworthy partner that will supply you with all the necessary information you need to function in a positive and creative manner. Meditation is a key element in tapping into your creative power and imagination. Remember, thought energy will flow to and through you as long as you are relaxed and your "Energy" hose is unkinked.

We said that your subconscious responds according to the beliefs and convictions held in your consciousness. Your conscious mind chooses what it believes to be true, and your subconscious accepts without question whatever it dictates. Your subconscious will accept failure as readily as success; it is, in fact, the means that will bring about either one.

At this very moment, your subconscious is working for or against you. Through your conscious mind, it senses and records all of your physical, intellectual, mental, and emotional experiences and stores the information for further use. The sum total of these experiences determines your present level of awareness.

As we've said, our conscious minds are greatly influenced by our five senses, so it is easy to see why we get confused when we use the conscious mind alone to bring about the right answers to our challenges. The five senses do not report the truth to us most of the time, so we accept, reject, and relate everything based on a distorted view of reality. To look at a situation and evaluate the information with the conscious mind alone is to look at the effect instead of the cause. This makes us value-judge both others and ourselves and evaluate what we see, hear and feel as if it were the truth. The lives of so many people are plagued with one obstacle after another because they take actions and make decisions based on false awareness. James Earl Jones, for example, had a terrible speech impediment as a child but instead of succumbing to it, he overcame his stuttering and now has one of the most distinctive and recognizable voices in the world.

What we need to do is to train ourselves to look within and ask our subconscious mind for guidance. As long as we rely on the conscious mind alone, we will continue to make mistakes and become disappointed and frustrated. There is a tremendous power in words. Words can build or destroy your life. They made you what you are right now. Words are verbalized thinking. You utter approximately twenty-five thousand of them each day. The way you talk to yourself has a profound effect on your feelings, actions, and accomplishments. What you say determines practically everything you do. Your words can change your blood pressure, heartbeat, and breathing. Indeed, James Earl Jones, who was ridiculed as a child, now makes his living from the very words that were once his difficulty.

The subconscious accepts without question the words we use, whether they are positive or negative. Positive statements or affirmations build your life while negative statements or affirmations destroy it. Take a moment right now to think about whether you use any of these negative and self-deprecating statements.

1. I am not talented.
2. I'll never be able to get in shape.
3. I don't have time.
4. I can't change.
5. That's the way I am.
6. I'm not perfect.
7. I can't do this.

Of course, the list could go on and on, but it is enough to show you how we program ourselves. Your subconscious doesn't know anything different than what it is told, so these negative messages become a part of our thought processes. This self-sabotaging mindset puts a halt to our creativity and limits our imagination. We experience sickness, lack, limitation, and failure.

What you must do is monitor your speech and turn such self-defeating statements around. The way to program your mind is to use our Mind Muscle Exercises and repeat them over and over again until your subconscious accepts them as reality. In psychology, this is called the Law of Predominant Mental Impression. When you keep saying that you aren't graceful or coordinated, your subconscious has no option but to make you that way; instead, if you affirm balance and harmony, your subconscious will make certain that is how you are. Never rehearse an adverse situation by saying to yourself that you feel great, only to tell the next person who asks how you are that you "feel terrible" just to get their sympathy. Switching back and forth only confuses the subconscious, and this will have repercussions in your life.

Emotion is the cornerstone of creativity. No creative act is performed without it. The subconscious responds greatly to feelings and emotions. Repetition by itself has little effect, but a word of caution: negative emotions and feelings, such as F.A.D. (fear, anxiety and doubt), work with just as much force as their positive counterparts. This is why they are so destructive.

Speaking or listening to music while using repetition increases the intensity of the vibrations and helps impress the information in your subconscious more quickly. Psychological studies have shown that using soothing music or voice recordings increases this speed by as much as 85 percent.

Everything starts in the mind. It is imperative to understand this. Imagination or visualization is the picturing power of your mind. Your subconscious responds to pictures and images held on your mental screen. Your subconscious is the choreographer that creates your life. You are the dancer, and your imagination and creativity is the routine.

Once you visualize the life you want, your desires will become reality. You are a self-fulfilling prophecy. What you are thinking about today is a clear indication of what you will experience in the future. Remember though— you have to be realistic; physical limitations need to be factored into your visualizations. Your thoughts of yesterday are what determined your results of today just as the thoughts of today will determine the results of tomorrow. If you truly want different results for the future, you have to change your thoughts now.

Visualize yourself having, doing, or being what you want. Feel yourself enjoying them. See the details—colors, places, and people—as vividly as you can. Hold the pictures clearly in your mind. Most important—you must put you in the picture. Get yourself a scrapbook and call it your "Blueprint of Destiny." In it, put colored pictures of the things you want, the places you want to go, or the things you want to do. Look at the pictures every day. Let them seep into your subconscious. Soon, you will master the technique of visualization; in the process, your desire will become your reality. You will create cells of recognition of the images you imagined that will be permanently implanted in your sub-conscious.

You can train your subconscious to perform any act you consciously choose. When a great athlete performs with ease, you can be sure that he or she has spent years building habit-patterns of perfection in their subconscious. Their subconscious mind stores these memories and releases them under automatic control, so that he or she does not have to consciously think which muscle to use each time they compete. It is the same with the martial arts. Muscle memory is developed through repetition and practice. The goal is that the martial arts practitioner reacts instinctively and not consciously so their techniques are executed with lightning speed.

Your subconscious is automatic and provides solutions to obstacles. It is never limited because it can be trained and retrained. Just as long as you keep on picturing what you want, it will forget mistakes, change course, correct itself, and bring you right on target, all automatically. The key to tapping into your subconscious power is to foster the feeling that it's working. You must, therefore, picture the end result. Visualize that you can get what you want. It is already yours. Experience the enjoyment and the excitement now.

Your limiting, conscious mind may conspire against you through your intellect. It may tell you your desires cannot be achieved; that they're impossible. (Remember the X Factor?) Do not accept this as the truth. Instead, remember you will get what you want when you feel as though you already have it.

{ Every great advance in science has issued from a new audacity of the imagination.

—JOHN DEWEY }

Shifting From the Comparative to the Creative Plane

Is it possible to find success without comparing yourself to others? The answer to that could provide considerable insight into many aspects of your life. When we understand the philosophy behind creation, and when we truly leave the comparative plane for the creative plane, then we become free. When you are in a constant state of comparison, then you are by necessity on guard. We like to say that it is better to focus your energy on what you want rather then spending your time comparing. For example, a martial arts school opened up right down the street from Chris's martial arts school. His first inclination was comparative. He was worried and concerned that they would try to take his clients and students out from under him. After about a day of this thought pattern he shifted to the creative plane. Chris realized that this other school was not a concern at all and that he would spend his energy on the development of his students and expansion of martial arts in the community. The outcome; Chris's school continues to flourish while the other school was forced to close down. Chris continued on the Creative Plane and the other school was definitely on the Comparative Plane, which didn't go so well for them.

When we move from the comparative to the creative plane, then we know that there are no limitations to what we can achieve. We are no longer consumed with the thought of protecting our property, our ideas, or ourselves. We no longer need to keep our eye on the competition. We are free to share and cooperate with others. Few have ever achieved true success by duplicating others. Two people can take the exact same action, and one may find great success while the other fails miserably.

> 66 In my industry, I never compare myself to others. I'm only aware of my own capabilities and talents. I utilize my own creative process to create my own business. I feel that I don't have any competition. When I first meet a prospective client, I want them to get inside my head to understand our philosophy about money and our planning methodology. I imagine them already as a client and visualize our long-lasting business relationship; I see how I not only have made a tremendous impact on their lives but also know that they will be in a better place because of me. My level of awareness is that the client has already experienced success. This gives off positive energy to the prospective client. They want to work with me even if they don't truly understand our process fully. 99
>
> —NICK

Imagination Exercise

In a quiet room, close your eyes and imagine the ocean. Now seat yourself on the beach and imagine smelling the sea breeze in the air. Taste the salt. Feel the grains of sand with your fingers. Watch the waves roll back and forth over the shore. Listen to seagulls flying through the air. Can you see the waves crashing against the shore? Do you feel like you are truly there? What else do you see? Are you hot, cold, calm, or relaxed? Did the exercise transport you to another place? Did you truly feel as if you were sitting on the beach in front of the ocean? Now instead of the ocean, imagine whatever it is you desire most in this life.

CHAPTER SUMMARY

- Imagination separates us from all other species.
- Imagination is the offspring of our thoughts.
- Imagination takes you off auto-pilot.
- Worthy Ideals arise from imagination.
- Break "out of the box" and create your own reality.
- Imagination is the greatest force in the universe.
- Our conscious mind limits us to the outside world.
- Our subconscious mind, if programmed correctly, has no boundaries.
- Imagination requires us to think with our IQ.
- To unleash our imagination, we must shift from the comparative plane to the creative plane.

CHAPTER THIRTEEN

Organized Planning

{
Success is the progressive realization of a worthy ideal.

—EARL NIGHTINGALE
}

The previous twelve chapters taught you the techniques of the T.R.A.N.S.F.O.R.M.A.T.I.O.N. Doctrine. Now we want to arm you with a plan of action to apply these methods to your life as we have ours. This chapter is so important, we would like you to read it over and over again. Just as repetition penetrates your subconscious, so will the words and exercises in this chapter (as well as the previous ones) do the same.

We feel so strongly about repetition and committing your T.R.A.N.S.F.O.R.M.A.T.I.O.N. Doctrine to paper that we will be asking you to redo one exercise from each of the previous twelve chapters. To assist you with this task, each of the chapter summaries are restated below. We will also ask you to write a new I AM statement that coincides with each chapter.

Chapter 1—Thought

- We are all born with the same intellectual qualities to succeed.
- Your thoughts can alter the chemicals in your brain.
- You have complete control over your conscious mind.
- Any thought you repeat is automatically accepted into your subconscious mind.
- Your thoughts shape your reality.
- The conscious mind has the ability to accept, reject, or neglect any thought.
- Your conscious mind is your thinking mind.
- Your subconscious mind can only accept what it is given by your conscious mind.
- Your subconscious mind is your emotional or feeling mind.
- Empowered Mastery's Success Formula: Thoughts determine how you feel; how you feel determines your actions; your actions ultimately determine your results.
- So if you want to change the results in your life, start changing your thoughts.

YOU ARE THE PICASSO OF YOUR LIFE

Chapter 2—Replacing Emotional Scars

- At a very young age, our thoughts were formed by those who were most influential in our lives.
- Paradigms and limiting beliefs control the results in your life.
- Replacing negative thoughts with productive and encouraging thoughts paves the road for improvement and success in life.
- Obstacles and setbacks in life are eliminated through T.R.A.N.S.F.O.R.M.A.T.I.O.N. of your thought process.
- Understanding the X/Y Factor of your mind is key to achieving any goal that you set for yourself.

PARALYZING PARADIGMS
Example. I am too old to begin that exercise program.

1.

2.

3.

4.

POWER PARADIGMS
Example. I AM healthy and vital and am in the best shape of my life!

1.

2.

3.

4.

Chapter 3—Awareness

- The level of awareness you are currently living in dictates your current status in life.
- Everyone is born with the same IQ's to succeed in life.
- Stress and tension prevent you from attaining a high state of awareness.
- You need to think beyond your five senses and use your intellectual qualities.

These include:

- Imagination
- Confidence
- Optimism
- Desire (burning)
- Passion
- Commitment
- Faith
- Vision
- Living Through Your Worthy Ideal

IN THE SPACE BELOW, REFLECT ON YOUR LIFE AND DESCRIBE TIMES WHEN YOUR LEVEL OF AWARENESS WAS AT ITS PEAK AND WHY.

1.
2.
3.

REWRITE YOUR LAB REPORT:

Worthy Ideal Statement:

Life Purpose Statement:

Core Four Areas of Life:

Top Five Goals:

Chapter 4—Never Give Up

- Persistence empowers you to overcome obstacles and challenges.
- Will pushes you to strive for the best you can be.
- A burning desire is more than just a want in life.
- Successful people persist while others walk away.
- Without a burning desire, persistence is just a word.

WRITE A SCENARIO IN YOUR LIFE WHERE YOU USED PERSISTENCE TO ACCOMPLISH A GOAL.

Chapter 5—Self-Image

- A positive self-image is easily developed once we stop comparing ourselves to others.
- As self-image improves, so does confidence.
- Use "I AM" statements to affirm your positive self-image.
- Visualize the image you want and firmly plant it in your subconscious mind.
- A firm, positive self-image enables you to take on more responsibilities.

	What is your current self image regarding...	How do you want to improve your self image regarding...
Your physical appearance?		
Your family		
Your friends		
Your career		

Chapter 6—Focus

- Focus unleashes trapped creative energy.
- A strong belief along with a positive attitude can help you to overcome illness.
- Self-control increases your ability to focus.
- Self-control helps you to react to situations in a calm manner.
- The scientific act and the art of focusing are absolutely vital to your success.
- Focus on what you want.
- Focus on progress, not perfection.

LIST THE AREAS OF YOUR LIFE IN ORDER OF IMPORTANCE.

1.

2.

3.

4.

5.

6.

7.

8.

9.

10.

11.

12.

13.

14.

REWRITE YOUR CORE FOUR AND THREE ACTION STEPS

1:_____

action step:

action step:

action step:

2:_____

action step:

action step:

action step:

3:_____

action step:

action step:

action step:

4:_____

action step:

action step:

action step:

Chapter 7—Opportunities

- There are no such things as problems—just challenges.
- No negative event or circumstance should prevent you from achieving your goals.
- Stop focusing on obstacles. Instead focus on how they can be of benefit to you.
- Conquering your challenges paves the road to success.
- Adversity reveals your true character.
- Mistakes are inevitable. Successful people respond to mistakes as learning experiences.

LIST THE CHALLENGES YOU ARE CURRENTLY FACING. FIND THE OPPORTUNITY IN EACH.

CHALLENGE	OPPORTUNITY
Example: $75,000 in two days	Create lifetime memberships
1.	
2.	
3.	
4.	
5.	
6.	
7.	
8.	
9.	
10.	

Chapter 8—Realization

- Before you can live your Life's Purpose, you must first realize and discover your Worthy Ideals.
- Your Life's Purpose is how you want to be remembered and is your legacy left behind to loved ones.
- Live in the "be" mode of life.
- You will be remembered for who you are and not for your material possessions.
- Review your actions in life. Do they match your Worthy Ideal? Do they enable you to live according to your Life's Purpose?

IMPROVED WORTHY IDEAL:

LIFE'S PURPOSE:

Chapter 9—Meditation

- Tapping into a higher power gives you unlimited energy.
- Meditation unlocks the subconscious mind and enables you to tap into a higher power.
- Stress and tension have detrimental impacts on your life; meditation is one of the best methods to eliminate them.
- Breathing is a common cause for many ailments we suffer in life. It helps to maintain a state of calmness and relaxation.
- Most people don't breathe correctly.
- Meditation is the best form of mental exercise.

MEDITATION EXERCISE

First close your eyes, sit up straight and focus on your breathing. Count each breath as you inhale and exhale. Relax your mind and body as you clear all thoughts and images that come to you. Once you are totally relaxed, think of a future event in your life. Visualize this event, replaying the successful outcome over and over. Get emotionally attached to this picture as if it is already happening. Zoom in on the picture. See yourself and those around you. See it in color and up close. Now place yourself looking out at everything and everyone around you, as if you were really experiencing the event now. Feel the feelings of having or experiencing this event now. Ask yourself how this makes you feel. Take a mental snapshot of that image and store it in your mind so you can access that image at any point in time.

Chapter 10—Attitude

- Your attitude reflects the results you get in life.
- Positive attracts positive.
- Your attitude is a combination of your thoughts, feelings, and actions.
- Be in control of your emotions. Don't be an Emotional Puppet.
- Become a good finder.
- Surround yourself with those who share your outlook on life.
- Be grateful.

LIST TEN PEOPLE YOU SPEND THE MOST TIME WITH.	WHAT IS THEIR ATTITUDE?	HOW DOES IT AFFECT YOUR ATTITUDE?
1.		
2.		
3.		
4.		
5.		
6.		
7.		
8.		
9.		
10.		

Chapter 11—Track Your Goals

- Start setting goals one at a time.
- Prioritize your goals.
- COMMIT.
- Make sure your goals are aligned with your Worthy Ideal.
- Worthy Ideal, Life's Purpose, Areas of Life, Goals

WRITE DOWN YOUR TOP FIVE GOALS THAT ARE DIRECTLY RELATED TO YOUR WORTHY IDEAL:

Chapter 12—Imagination

- Imagination separates us from all other species.
- Imagination is the offspring of our thoughts.
- Imagination takes you off auto-pilot.
- Worthy Ideals arise from imagination.
- Break "out of the box" and create your own reality.
- Imagination is the greatest force in the universe.
- Our conscious mind limits us to the outside world.
- Our subconscious mind, if programmed correctly, has no boundaries.
- Imagination requires us to think with our IQ.
- To unleash our imagination, we must shift from the comparative plane to the creative plane.

LIFE SCRIPT STATEMENT

You are constantly running a mental movie with yourself as star of the show. These images determine your personal behavior and the kind of life you lead. You have the power to mentally create a new life for yourself. Whatever you visualize, you can have. All you must do is imagine yourself as having achieved your desire. Rewrite your Life Script Statement as if anything was possible. Imagine you were the producer, director, and main star of your life story. How do you want your life to be?

CHAPTER FOURTEEN

The New You

> Who I am today speaks far greater than
> what anyone can say about me. I thank
> God every day that I am alive and that I am
> able to dedicate my life to teaching others,
> enriching lives and acting as a vehicle for
> empowerment.
>
> **—TOM MALIN**

In Chapter 13, you found that your answers to our Conditioning for Success Exercises may have improved from before. Think back over the past ten years of your life, do you act the same way? Do you associate with the same people? How different are you now? We must constantly strive to better ourselves. In the introduction, we mentioned what separated our company, Empowered Mastery, from others. We also told you how this book would be different as well. Perhaps you weren't sure but were enticed enough not only to spend your hard earned dollars on this book but also to read it to this point. For that we thank you. But we don't want to rest on our laurels.

While reading this book, some of you may have thought about the enormous difference between knowing something and mastering it. In any profession or occupation, people achieve mastery by repetition until actions become automatic in the subconscious mind. Recall the sales person in Chapter 4 who has to make a certain amount of calls per week or appointments per day to make a sale. This is Sales 101 but very few salespeople are able to consistently apply and master this concept on a weekly basis. The same applies to our T.R.A.N.S.F.O.R.M.A.T.I.O.N. Doctrine. Even though you have read it once, twice, or several times, actually knowing, applying, and mastering the principles in this book is a whole new ballgame. Therefore, we want to take what we have written to the highest level possible and demonstrate to you how to put it to actual use. We can almost assure you that in this chapter we will take you to a new level other books rarely dare to venture.

One of my coaching clients a few years back was a very successful financial planner. He was also an avid reader of literature on personal development, and was excited to take our coaching program. During one of our first coaching calls, I started to teach him about our tools and philosophies. He interrupted me by saying, 'This is not first rodeo, I know all about these concepts!' I then very calmly challenged him by asking him, 'Are you applying them each day in your daily life?' There was a moment of silence as I could almost hear him thinking. He then simply answered, 'No.' That person was John Cammarano, who is now a valuable member of Embowered Mastery.

As martial artists our lives are predicated on character, discipline, and a specific way of life. We are far from perfect and are on a continuous journey for self-improvement, but we feel by teaching this information, it helps us improve our mindset, too. We would like to now share with you the step-by-step conditioning exercises we do on a daily basis. The outline of the "New You" Conditioning Exercises contained here may be overwhelming for some people. That's okay. Do whatever is most comfortable at your own pace. However, we strongly recommend that you try your best to push yourself to new levels;

after all, isn't that what achievement is all about? So stay with us and open your mind.

The following Mind Muscle Exercises are like lifting weights or working out for physical muscles. You wouldn't decide to get in shape by exercising for one week and then say, "Wow, I'm healthy" and stop working out. On the other hand, you might already be physically fit, but once you stop working out the muscles you've developed will start to disintegrate. The same applies to your mind. Your mind is the most powerful muscle you have. Every single day you must do exercises that condition it for success. Get to the point where performing these Mind Muscle Exercises is as much a part of your lifestyle as brushing your teeth. We suggest you choose a few to start with and then add more as you gain confidence.

Fourteen Conditioning Steps for Success

Say Thank You and I Love You. Say "thank you" as soon as you wake up and continue to say it twenty times. Then look at yourself in the mirror, smile, and say, "Today is a great day to be alive." Give thanks for being alive, for seeing another day, for being with the people you love the most, and for breathing the air around you. As soon as you turn off the alarm, tell those close to you that you love them.

See Your Goal. Then read your goal card out load and look at your vision. If you haven't created your vision board yet, place a corresponding picture that aligns with your goal on a piece of paper or cardboard. It can be a car, a home, a specified amount of money, or a photo of the body that you want to have. Every morning make your goal the first image you see. Become emotionally attached to it and let your goal be the fuel to energize you at the start of each day.

Drink Water. Drink a glass of water with lemon. Your body needs to hydrate itself after fasting. That's why it's called break-fast. In the morning, you are breaking your fast of not eating during your sleep. Your body is made up of approximately 70 percent water. You'll immediately feel energized after drinking water because it's what your organs need to function. But don't just drink any water. Yes, we know that you might be saying to yourself that all water is the same, right? But you would be mistaken; there are five levels of waters:

5. Tap water. Almost all tap water has chemicals and toxins that aren't good for your body.

4. Filtered tap water. This is water in filtered jugs in any convenience stores.

3. Bottled waters. Not all bottled waters are created equal. Look for bottled water that states the pH level on the bottle. For example, Fiji water has a pH of 7.5.

2. Reverse osmosis filtering system that you can put in your home.

1. Distilled water. You can buy at any health food store.

Power Breathing. Start your morning with a focused breathing exercise instead of drinking that first cup of coffee. Your body can go days without water but only seconds without breathing. Oxygen supplies energy to the body. There is a direct correlation between your health and the level of oxygen in your bloodstream. So inhale for four counts and then exhale for a four count while walking. You will notice a difference as your body wakes up, especially after drinking water.

Grateful Statements. Most people focus on all they lack in their life instead of what they have. State out loud everything you are grateful for. Try starting with five things. For example: I am grateful for my health, I am grateful for my family, I am grateful for my home, I am grateful for the food I eat, and I am grateful for the air I breathe. Almost anyone can use at least one of these examples to begin their day. This exercise will automatically condition you to become a good finder. The power of gratitude eliminates any negativity within your life. Once you think, feel, and state what you are grateful for, you will attract more positivity into your life. Think back to the Dr. Emoto experiment. Imagine what's crystallizing in you as soon as you drink your water and say your power words of gratitude.

Rebounding. In the morning after you've completed the above steps, jump on a mini trampoline for five minutes. Regular lymphasizing increases the flow of lymphatic fluid throughout the body, feeds your cells and produces energy. Rebounding also is the most effective way to stimulate the immune system and increase internal cleansing to the cellular level. This balances the kinetic energy in the muscles, making you feel revitalized and reenergized. If you don't have a mini trampoline, consider purchasing one or jump rope as a substitute.

Gratitude Journal. Keep a gratitude journal. Write in it every morning. A good place to keep this is in the bathroom. As long as you're in there, you might as well make the most of your time. Begin your grateful statement with "I am thankful for..." and begin your grateful intentions with "I am grateful now that...." Writing your statements in the present tense will send messages not only to your subconscious mind but also to the world around us.

Meditation. Meditation is your natural resource for health and has enormous benefits. It increases oxygen and blood circulation, strengthens internal organs, improves digestion, builds your immune system, balances hormones, quiets the nervous system, calms the mind, and increases energy levels.

> Sit in a crossed-leg or lotus position with your back and neck straight. You may want to use a meditation pillow. If not, you can sit on a chair. The lotus position may be difficult at first, however, after some practice your body will adjust and you will find it more comfortable Make sure to keep your back straight and place one hand on top of the other, palms up and thumbs interlocked. The hands should be about two inches below your belly button. The main purpose for meditation is to focus on breathing and to quiet our minds to tap into higher energy sources.

Paradigm Conditioning. Reconditioning your paradigms, or experiencing paradigm shifts, is not a one-time event. It must be reinforced on a daily basis. So much of what we talk about in this book is repetitive because that is the only way to make an imprint on your subconscious mind. In life, we constantly strive to improve, so we must make room for those new thought processes. Repeat your new Power Paradigm statements five times.

Life's Purpose Statement. Repeat your Life's Purpose statement aloud. This practice embeds it into your subconscious and also puts it in your awareness for the rest of the day. You should repeat this statement often enough that it becomes second nature. You should be able to repeat it as easily as your phone number.

"I AM" Statements. Making "I AM" statements is one of our favorite Mind Muscle exercises. The words "I AM" will be extremely powerful every time you attach them to a statement, but the goal is to choose a series of qualities that you want to have or that align with the person you want to become. It must support your Life's Purpose, Worthy Ideal, and goals.

Life Script Statements. In Chapter 11, we asked you to be a director and producer by writing your Life Script. Now we want you to be the star of the movie by reciting that Life Script with passion, belief, and conviction.

Stretch. If you've ever watched an animal wake up, what is the first thing they do? Stretching is the natural instinct in most animals. Take a look at your dog or cat. Why do they do this; are they smarter than us? An inflexible body is a result of an inflexible mind. Stretch. This loosens your muscles and eases tension. At our retreats, we teach people how to do certain stretches or energy exercises every morning as soon as they wake up. They are the same ones that our grand master has taught us. Perhaps you can even take a martial arts or yoga class to help you learn how to stretch and be more flexible.

Power Song and Mind Muscle Recording. On your way to work in the morning listen to a song that motivates and inspires you. This is a great way to start your day. Paul listens to U2's "Beautiful Day" to energize him for the day. Another song might be the theme from Rocky. Every time you hear your Power Song, you'll feel like going out and doing something productive and energizing. Take all the Mind Muscle statements that you say every morning and create a playlist. As you drive, you will have your Power Song, Grateful Statements, Power Paradigms, Life Script Statements, Life's Purpose Statements, and "I am" Statements with you. Play this Mind Muscle recording every morning and evening with any other series of empowering statements. These recordings should be in your own voice.

As we mentioned earlier, don't let these overwhelm you. We don't expect you to wake up one morning and do everything. Crawl before you walk and walk before you run. Start slow and build upon each one. This may take you out of your comfort zone, but this is what success is all about. Don't expect results overnight. Remember, it takes twenty-one days to make or break a habit. This is a process so let your life evolve with these Mind Muscle Exercises.

Until we see you at one of EMC retreats or seminars, we would like you to take our T.R.A.N.S.F.O.R.M.A.T.I.O.N. Challenge. In the diagram below, we've included a seven-month pyramid. Each month take on two new conditioning steps. By the end of the seven months, you will have successfully completed all fourteen steps as a part of your daily routine. At the end of this challenge, the reward is a new you! What can you accomplish with this new sense of empowerment? How much better will your new life be? How many people will benefit from your transformation? The only one stopping you is you. We would love to hear your successful results, please email us at info@empoweredmastery.com. And remember, you have Infinite Power!

The New You!

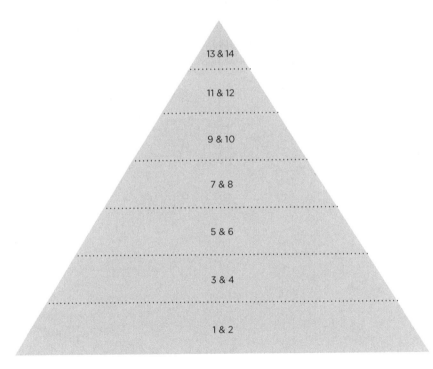

13 & 14

11 & 12

9 & 10

7 & 8

5 & 6

3 & 4

1 & 2

CONCLUSION

Before we get to our personal acknowledgements, we would like to personally thank you, the reader. We are extremely honored and privileged to have the opportunity to write this book, and to share our principles and philosophies with you. We realize that there is a wealth of information in our T.R.A.N.S.F.O.R.M.A.T.I.O.N. Doctrine, and that some of you might have had to empty your cup. However, we know with all our heart that this book will help you live a happier, healthier, and wealthier life. To show our appreciation and gratitude to you, we would love to have you attend the many seminars and programs that we host. Please visit our website www.empoweredmastery. com. There is a wealth of information about us, Empowered Mastery, and our programs, as well as free video content. Better yet, email us at info@ empoweredmastery.com. We would love to hear from you, and promise to answer all emails. Thank you for allowing us to live through our Worthy Ideal.

ACKNOWLEDGMENTS

I would like to acknowledge my loving wife, my rock, Linda, and my two beautiful children, Joseph and Lia, for your unconditional love and support. You are all God's greatest gift to me.

I would like to acknowledge my mom and dad for teaching me about values, dedication, and commitment. You are truly the greatest parents a man could ever ask for.

I would like to acknowledge my brother, Tony, for always being by my side. Through our loss, our bond grew stronger, and I thank you.

I would like to acknowledge my business partner, Scott Tasch, and the rest of the Opus Team, for the huge success in my career and for holding down the fort while I focused on the book.

I would like to acknowledge my partners and friends, Rick, Paul, and Chris, at Empowered Mastery for sharing the vision and the passion.

I would like to acknowledge the Saturday Men's Fellowship for your spiritual guidance, hope, and inspiration every week.

I would like to acknowledge Master Paul Melella, Master Anthony Melella, and Master Chris Berlow, not only for teaching Joseph and me the art of Taekwondo but also for giving balance to my life and sharing the bond with my son all these years.

—Nick

You Have Infinite Power is a culmination of both life experiences and philosophies that encourage everyone to believe that they have infinite potential and can accomplish anything in life. There are many people I would like to acknowledge who helped to create this book. They are not listed in order of importance but have all had a profound impact on who I am today and the philosophies in this book.

Kathy Berlow: My wife of over twenty years—her positive attitude and self-lessness have carried us throughout our lives. Her support for all of our endeavors is instrumental to every success we experience. I am very fortunate to live with my best friend. I love her tremendously and am very proud to share a life with her.

Brandon, Timmy, Kimberly, Andrew, and Stefanie: My children—they have had a profound effect on why I do what I do. One of my biggest driving forces is to show them that if they have a dream they desire, then they can achieve it! I want to be an inspiration for them to see that dreams do come to reality. I love them all tremendously, and they mean the world to me.

Curt Delano: my father—I could not adequately express the respect and appreciation I feel for him. My father is solely responsible for teaching me how to work hard and have fun doing it. His work ethic and knowledge will influence generations for years to come. I love him very much.

John Berlow, Lynda Gustavsen, Amanda Williamson: My brother and sisters—it is amazing how we all stay extremely close even though all of us, except John, live so far apart. I am extremely grateful to have such a loving, caring family, and look forward to a lifetime of laughs and fun. Love you guys.

Grandmaster Kim, Grandmaster Ed Ciarfella, and Master Joe Badini: my Taekwondo family—I am so grateful and appreciative for the guidance, leadership, and friendship from all of you. I am the person and the martial artist I am today because of all of you. I am eternally grateful for that. *Cam sa ham ni dah.*

My United Martial Arts Centers team and students—I could not do what I do if it wasn't for all of you. Thanks for seeing the big picture and the vision and allowing me to have the freedom to run.

Last but definitely not least: to my EMC partners, Rick, Paul, and Nick— it is awesome to share the vision we have, and it is an honor to work with such positive, energetic, and motivated individuals.

—Chris

I believe that there are no accidents in this universe. Everything is designed for growth, evolution, and improvement. There was a reason why Empowered Mastery was formed and why we as a team came together to organize this information into the T.R.A.N.S.F.O.R.M.A.T.I.O.N. Doctrine. As this book transformed from an idea into a physical form, I would like to express my deepest gratitude to the following:

First to God, who I believe is the Creative Source. There is an energy that comes to me and through me every time I speak and am in a position of influence to serve others. I truly believe that this energy is all around us and that we all have the ability to tap into our Creative Source. I am extremely grateful for that awareness.

Next, to all the mentors and teachers I have had in my life:

To my selfless and loving parents, Paul Melella Sr., the hardest worker I know, and Valerie Melella, a true mother who puts her children first. You both were my very first teachers and mentors. You gave me the foundation, belief, and love I needed to succeed in life.

Dad, thank you so much for teaching me the true meaning of life. You always told me that you were never financially wealthy, but you were wealthy with family and your five children were your treasure. You always worked really hard to provide for your family, and you made it happen. No matter how many challenges you were faced with, you always had a smile on your face. You taught me to treat others with respect and that there is another side to every story. Everyone who knows you loves you, and so do I.

Mom, you always told me how you knew that, whatever I did, I would be successful. There were times when I put you through some difficult situations and maybe had you think twice about that comment. No matter how many times I disappointed you or had to have you "go to bat" for me, you always loved me unconditionally. You are a true example of a mother and continue to selflessly care for all your children and grandchildren. You will always be the Grand Master, and I love you.

To Grand Master Byung Min Kim, for teaching me the "way." Without your guidance in meditation and Dah Do, I would not have been able to raise my level of awareness. I am deeply appreciative to have you as a spiritual guide toward enlightenment.

To Grand Master Edmund Ciarfella, for your belief and vision as a martial arts professional. You helped me see the light when it came to martial arts philosophy.

To Master Joseph Badini, for your continued friendship and support in everything that I do. You are my older brother and my longest friend in the martial arts.

To Master Paul Edwards, for your unconditional love and support as a friend. I am grateful to share magical moments with our families.

To all my team members at the United Martial Arts Centers of Carmel, New York, without your dedication, loyalty, commitment, and support, this book could not have been completed. Most specifically, to my beautiful sister, Gina, my director of operations and personal assistant, you are the face everyone loves to see when they walk into our center, and you keep our systems in place. Thank you for being so patient with me.

To my brother, partner, and best friend, Anthony Melella, you are my protégé. The passion for making a difference has truly been passed down to you. I know that you love to impact the lives of others through martial arts. You allowed me to step away and live my Worthy Ideal and Life's Purpose at a higher level. Thank you for your support and continuous belief in everything we do.

To my UMAC team, Mrs. Schnaudigel, Mrs. Leifer, Paul Maglietta and Mrs. Maddock, all of you are influential to the success of our program. Your unconditional love and selflessness is beyond measure. I can't thank you enough for being my loyal "padawans."

To my sisters, Kathy Peverini and Dana Melella, for your laughter and love. You always make me feel special when you laugh at my jokes.

To my grandmother, "beautiful Rose," without your help I wouldn't have had a head start on life. I love you.

To my partners Chris Berlow, Nick Palumbo and Rick Wollman, I am truly grateful to share our vision and Worthy Ideal together. It is refreshing to surround myself with successful people that do not have any egos and respect others' abilities, strengths and talents. You all have helped me become a better person.

To my loving wife Gina, my "little bootie" Kiahna Isabel, and my "little Buddy," Pierce Michael Melella. For those fourteen-hour days when I would be out of the house first traveling to corporations for Empowered Mastery in the morning and then teaching for United Martial Arts Centers at night, and for those weekends when I was away either writing, teaching, or speaking, thank you for loving, supporting, and appreciating the fact that I am put on earth to serve others and to make a difference in the world. I am truly living this Worthy

Ideal to lead by example and to provide a shift of mindset for our family. You are the driving force in everything I do, and my world revolves around the love I have for all of you.

Finally to all my UMAC students, EMC clients, and to you, the reader. I thank you all for allowing me to serve you by teaching classes, giving seminars and retreats, and most of all, by writing this book. I love teaching this information. Without you, I would not be able to live my Worthy Ideal. Thank you for allowing us to share the T.R.A.N.S.F.O.R.M.A.T.I.O.N. Doctrine with you.

—Paul

I would like to thank my wife, Sharon, who took me from the abyss of despair to the apex of happiness. She shined a light at the end of the tunnel where I only saw darkness. She taught me the true meaning of love and all the pleasures that come with it. She is my best friend, whom I look forward to sitting with on our front porch during our twilight years, holding hands and talking the night away.

I would like to thank my kids. Spencer, who is now 17, has a knack for writing, a warm and caring heart, and tremendous insight and wisdom for someone of his age. Max just turned 21, and has a businessman's mentality. He shows signs of being a true entrepreneur. Justin is 22 and has started his career in TV, working for NBC sports. He is mature and responsible beyond his years. Jessica, 24, is a patent researcher in NYC. She has overcome many challenges and is now thriving. She works harder than most adults and has a work ethic to match. I am so proud of all of you.

Finally, to my partners, friends, and coauthors, Chris, Nick, and Paul. I'd have to write another book just to describe how they have inspired and impacted my life. They have given me my Worthy Ideal.

—Rick

ABOUT THE AUTHORS

Nick Palumbo resides in Westchester County, New York, along with his wife, Linda, and their two children, Joseph and Lia. In his free time, Nick loves to golf, practice martial arts, and coach his children.

Paul Melella Jr. resides in Putnam County, New York, with his wife, Gina, and their two children, Kiahna Isabel and Pierce Michael. When he is not teaching martial arts, speaking at seminars, coaching corporations, or writing new material, he loves spending time with his family, mountain biking, snowboarding, hiking, weight lifting, and practicing martial arts and yoga.

Chris Berlow currently resides in Cortlandt Manor, New York, with Kathy, his wife of fifteen years, and their five children: Brandon, Andrew, Timmy, Stefanie, and Kimberly. He currently teaches martial arts at his school in Briarcliff Manor and continues to work hard with Nick, Paul, and Rick to bring the T.R.A.N.S.F.O.R.M.A.T.I.O.N. Doctrine to the world!

Rick Wollman lives in Rockland County, New York, with his wife, Sharon, and their four children, Spencer, Max, Justin, and Jessica, and the family's two dogs, Snickers and Shelby. He is an avid runner and sports enthusiast who loves spending time with his family.

INDEX

Made in the USA
Middletown, DE
07 December 2019

80197436R00156